SIAM IN MIND

DAVID K. WYATT

SILKWORM BOOKS

OTHER BOOKS BY DAVID K. WYATT

- *The Politics of Reform in Thailand* (1969)
- *Hikayat Patani: The Story of Patani* (with A. Teeuw)(2 vols., 1969)
- *In Search of Southeast Asia: A Modern History* (with David J. Steinberg et al., 1972; 2nd ed. 1988)
- *The Crystal Sands: The Chronicles of Nagara Sri Dharrmaraja* (1975)
- *The Short History of the Kings of Siam* (by Jeremias van Vliet [1640]; Edited; 1975)
- *Moral Order and the Question of Change: Essays on Southeast Asian Thought* (edited with Alexander Woodside; 1982)
- *Thailand: A Short History* (1984)
- *Temple Murals as an Historical Source* (1993)
- *Studies in Thai History* (1994)
- *The Nan Chronicle* (1994)
- *The Chiang Mai Chronicle* (with Aroonrut Wichienkeeo; 1995; 2nd ed. 1998)
- *Tamnan phün müang Chiang Mai* (with Aroonrut Wichienkeeo; 2000)
- *The Royal Chronicles of Ayutthaya* (tr. Richard Cushman; edited; 2000)
- *Siam in Mind* (2002)

ISBN 974–7551–72-1

First edition published in 2002 by
Silkworm Books
104/5 Chiangmai-Hot Road, T. Suthep, Muang, Chiang Mai 50200
E-mail: silkworm@pobox.com

Cover: Mural painting, Wat Phumin, Nan
Photograph: D. K. Wyatt
Set in 12 point HP-Garamond
Printed in Thailand by O. S. Printing House, Bangkok

to

Alene
Douglas
Andrew
James
John
Dick
Debbie
Penny

CONTENTS

PLATES

PREFACE

In early 2001, I attended a workshop in the Netherlands, and my paper for that occasion was distributed in advance like all the others, dealing with the definition of Southeast Asia. On my first night in Amsterdam, I suffered badly from every traveler's nightmare, and jet-lag awakened me at 3 A.M. As I lay sleeplessly awake, I decided that the paper I had written was inadequate, so I set about composing in my head an alternative paper. Twelve hours later, I delivered that alternate paper, basically arguing something like the Introduction to this volume.

A few days later, settling in to my airline seat for the trans-Atlantic trip, I decided to put my late-night ideas to the test, and in the next few hours I sketched a rough outline of what I hope amounts to something like an intellectual history of Thailand. My long-suffering publisher and good friend, Trasvin Jittidecharak, kindly agreed to let me put aside the book I had promised to write for her, and to write this one instead.

Many of the chapters in this volume might seem familiar to readers. That is because I continue to be puzzled and preoccupied by many things that have persisted over the years. On occasion I have copied quotations, but I always have refrained from quoting myself. And I should say something about the style of scholarship in this volume. I have been less rigorous in scholarly attribution of evidence than I would have preferred. Much of what I say is there as my opinion. I have been liberal in allowing my imagination to run freely, and I have stuck my neck out on a few points. Some things I have said might get me into trouble, and a few might even get me shot at. So be it. I certainly no longer have any illusions about my mortality.

I am indebted to the organizers of the Dutch workshop, Remco Rabin and Henk Schulte Nordholt, for their patience and understanding, and also for many old friends who were there, and were always good company. In particular, Baas Terwiel, Bernhard Dahm, Wim Wolters, Robert Cribb, and Han ten Brummelhuis. Many of them, in addition to providing good company, also took turns at pushing my wheelchair over the mercifully level streets of Amsterdam.

It has been genuine fun writing this book. I am grateful to those I could persuade to read and comment on these chapters, and also to those who could put up with my distraction. Here I am especially grateful to Tamara Loos, Barbara Andaya, David Chandler, David Joel Steinberg, and Tracie Matysik.

I remain eternally grateful to the doctors who saved my life in the first half of 1999, especially Adam Law and David Schwed. I could not have survived without them and without Alene, our three sons, and my two brothers and two sisters.

David K. Wyatt
Lansing, New York
6 August 2001

INTRODUCTION

WE ARE TOLD THAT JUST ABOUT EVERY REGION
of the world that is written about has an intellectual history.
We are not always told how that term might be defined, but
we are assured that the region's people had great thoughts that
have enriched the world. This seems to have been said about
nearly every part of the world except Southeast Asia. Lacking
any "intellectual history," the people of Southeast Asia, historians seem to be telling us, did not think, as if they somehow
lacked mental capacity, or were occupied instead with more
mundane affairs. Is it possible that, if "intellectual history" is
the study of thought and the products of thought, then the
people of Southeast Asia did not think? Can this be true?

I have been trying since at least 1977 to argue the contrary;
but I am left thinking that perhaps no one has been paying any
attention.[1] This slim book is an effort to try to argue the
contrary, at least for Siam or Thailand. If it does not meet the
usual definitions of what "intellectual history" might be, it
might instead be considered to be social history or cultural

---

1. David K. Wyatt, "Reflections on the Intellectual History of Pre-
Modern Southeast Asia," *Proceedings Seventh IAHA Conference, 22–26
August 1977*, Bangkok (Bangkok: Chulalongkorn University Press, 1977),
II, pp. 1576–1590; *Moral Order and the Question of Change: Essays on
Southeast Asian Thought* (ed. David K. Wyatt and Alexander Woodside;
New Haven: Yale University Southeast Asian Studies, 1982).

history, but in some way it has to do with what was going on inside the heads of a particular widely-defined group of Southeast Asians. I should hasten to add that similar books could be written about every region of Southeast Asia. I am not trying to write such a book because work like that is heavily dependent upon language skills which I lack.

"Intellectual history" as I have been defining it here has not merely to do with the history of "great thoughts" by "great thinkers." All kinds of thinking were being done by very ordinary people. Some of them were so "ordinary" that their names are not recorded, and in some cases their thoughts have become integrated into the everyday thinking of whole societies.

As mentioned earlier, "intellectual history" is the study of thought, and products of thought, through time. It is best defined to include not only the work of intellectuals, but also the thinking of all sorts of people. This book is intended to sample all kinds of thought over the past 1300 years, in many different regions of what we think of today as Thailand. I have tried to touch upon political and religious thought, but also upon such "artistic" thought as that demonstrated in novels, paintings, and historical writing. It includes both people whom we might think of as conservative and royalist, and also those who usually are thought of as non-conforming.

The emphasis, of course, is on what we might think of as intellectual; but at the same time I have tried to give the book a "spine" of historical comprehensiveness, so that most periods since about the ninth century are at least summarized. A more full historical sequence can be obtained by a reading of some more general account of Thai history, including the most recent edition of my somewhat misnamed *Thailand: A Short History* (Yale University Press and Silkworm Books, 1984).

2

"SILVER BULLET"

IN THE EARLY MONTHS OF THE YEAR 802, A PARTY of Cambodian men assembled atop a small mountain to the north of present-day Siem Reap and Angkor. Chief among this group was a man whom we would later know as Jayavarman II, who ruled over Angkorean Cambodia from 802 to 850 or thereabouts.

About this man and his friends we know little. We do know that he and (presumably) others were captured and taken as captives or hostages to the island of Java (which may be in present-day Indonesia) several decades earlier. Around 770, he made his way back to the lower regions of the Mekong River north of Prei Ving where he had relatives and friends, and where he was able to gather a group of followers and advisers. These he won to his side by proving his abilities as a leader, and by granting some of them lands and administrative power. Chief among these was a (non-Indian) Brahman called Sivakaivalya, who became his chaplain and chief among his advisors. Together, this group soon raided first the towns along the lower Mekong, next the towns to the northwest of the Great Lake (Tonle Sap), and then just east of that point, near and to the east of Angkor.[1]

---

1. I rather like the account by Claude Jacques (Cologne: Köndmann, 1999), pp. 43–44.

Jayavarman must have known that political chaos and incessant warfare had contributed to the region's weakness, and had brought about his own capture and exile to Java. At the same time, he might have been discouraged by the fact that many small principalities still lay unconquered to the north of the escarpment (that today marks the northern frontier of Cambodia). Unceasing warfare seemed still to surround him.

We don't know who got the word first—whether it was Jayavarman II or Sivakaivalya, or some other among the young king's advisors. But some among them heard that there was some learned man away off in the extreme northeast. That man was called Hirañadâma—literally "Silver Arrow," but we might refer to him as "Silver Bullet," after the ordnance used to slay malevolent creatures. "Silver Bullet" was offering such magic, at what price we do not know. He offered to teach Jayavarman II's chaplain some secret magic incantations that would make the king superior to all other kings on earth, including even the rulers of Java. This would have amounted to a break-through, and Jayavarman could hardly resist. A meeting was arranged for the summit of Phnom Kulen, just north of the location of Angkor.

At the appointed time, Hirañadâma arrived, probably alone, from Janapada, far away in the northeast. As a later inscription explains,

Then a brahman named Hiranyadama, an expert in magical science, came from Janapada[2] because His Majesty Para-meshvara had invited him to accomplish a supplementary ceremony so as to make it impossible for this country of Kambuja to be dependent on Java; and to

2. Perhaps Prasat Khna in Mlu Prei.

4

assert the existence of only one absolutely unique master over the land, who would be a cakravartin.[3]

He brought in his head, but not in his hands, four texts, the contents of which he taught for the memorization of Sivakaivalya. We might imagine that he recited these aloud, line by line, until the chaplain had memorized their whole. We might imagine that, at the same time, Sivakaivalya consecrated a small, portable bronze image that was to be the repository of the chants' words. And we are later told that wherever the king and his successors went, there the image (and the chants) went also.

We are never told that, when all was finished, "Silver Bullet" returned to Janapada. Nor are we told that "Silver Bullet" received any gift or payment for his services. We are left to conclude that, when the ceremony was concluded, "Silver Bullet" was killed. The manuscripts on which he had based his work disappeared, one of which was discovered by Teun Goudriaan only in the 1970s.[4]

The significance of what "Silver Bullet" did is that he seems to have inaugurated the formalities which made a king into a *devaraja*. And the importance of the *devaraja* idea is that it augmented a widespread cultural pattern in Southeast Asia which exaggerated the concept of royalty, making it possible to have only one "king" per realm, just as a family could have only one head, and even twins could not be equals and one had to be senior to the other.

3. A Universal Monarch, one whom all other kings must acknowledge as superior.
4. Teun Goudriaan, *The inasikhatantra* (New Delhi: Motilal Banarsidass, 1985), pp. 4–7. I am grateful to Wynn Willcox for finding this rare text and outlining its significance for me.

The other surprising thing about "Silver Bullet" and Janapada has to do with where this *devaraja* ceremony took place. Recent research shows not only that the Phnom Kulen mountain top was among other things a Buddhist site which had been consecrated for such rituals as ordinations, but also that the boundary stones implanted to delimit such ceremonies were very similar to such boundary stones (*sima*) as those known from Müang Fa Dæt in Kamalasai district of Kalasin province.[5]

Plates 1a & b — Buddhist boundary stones from Müang Fa Dæt
(left, photo Wyatt 1962)
and from Phnom Kulen (right, from Boulbet and Dagens)

5. J. Boulbet and B. Dagens, *Les sites archeologiques de la région du Bhnam Gulen* (Phnom Kulen) (Paris: Maisonneuve, 1973), p. 51, fn. 1.

WHY MIGHT the Phnom Kulen boundary stones have been like the Müang Fa Dæt stones? The most logical way of explaining this is to suggest that both were on important overland trading and communications routes. In this case, it might be equally interesting to see whether the concept of the *devaraja* was moving along these routes as well as the sculpting and statuary of Buddhist boundary stones. As we move in time down to the twelfth and thirteenth centuries, let's look for these.

Under ordinary circumstances, we would naturally divide history into "national" units; and the "Silver Bullet" story related above would be considered as a natural part of the history of Cambodia—or earlier, as part of the history of the kingdom of Angkor. But what happens when we include the Müang Fa Dæt element? We might suppose that the episode does not become a part of the history of Thailand until the Kamalasai area becomes a part of Thailand, after about 1777.

This still is not a very satisfactory solution. There is a better way of thinking about it. We might begin by thinking of the various ways in which different activities defined "zones" into which the landscape might have been divided. We might begin with economic exchanges, moving imported luxuries as well as imported ideas and fashions from the region at the head of the Gulf of Siam in northerly and northeasterly directions, traversing the Khorat Plateau and the Kalasin region, and converging on the Nakhon Phanom region. Gathering also the ceramics of the Songkhram River basin, traders went from there across the Mekong and up the Ca Dinh River to the Mu Gia Pass over the mountains to the Vinh area of central Vietnam. Salt and dried fish might also have been traded along this route, as also some metals (copper and tin), medicinals, and aromatic woods.

It is important to imagine this middle Mekong region not as

some empty space in between more active and economically rich areas, but as a region rich and important in its own right. After all, though some people might have profited from the carrying trade, moving commodities from one region to another, empty regions were not going to be major importers of religious ideas or builders of important religious monuments, the ruins of which dot the entire region.

Once we have in mind a more richly-textured image of the central portions of Indochina, including the Khorat Plateau, we are in a better position to imagine the movement of imported religious ideas, and art, and social organization. All three of these elements are pointed to by the Müang Fa Dæt and the Phnom Kulen sculptures. This was not simply a Khmer, or a Thai, or a Lao, zone. There were Vietnamese and Chinese, Mon and Indians, and numerous other ethnic groups present. So long as there were incentives for people to move about, then people—both men and women—were moving, and in the process their movement was enriching the life of the region.

RELICS

BY THE TWELFTH CENTURY, SHIPS WERE MOVING directly across the Bay of Bengal between ports on the Malay Peninsula and ports in southern India and adjacent parts of the island of Ceylon (Sri Lanka). They may have been carrying some commodities like gold, ceramics, and rare spices, or carrying out piratical raids, but they also were often carrying, in both directions, men bound on religious missions. As they had for several centuries, they may have been carrying what amounted to Buddhist missionaries, but increasingly they were carrying young Buddhist monks from Southeast Asia intending to study and be re-ordained in Sri Lanka. Some of these were to become established in Sri Lanka as famous scholars who wrote texts to be studied in the Buddhist world for some centuries—monks like Dhammakitti, author of an important history of a tooth-relic of the Lord Buddha. Most, however, soon returned to Southeast Asia with a renewed commitment to Buddhism and a heightened appreciation of its doctrines.

Travelers, merchants, and monks probably sailed directly across the Bay of Bengal from Sri Lanka (Ceylon) to the port of Trang. There they were loaded onto elephants, or joined horse caravans, for the gentle trip overland through the lush forests to Nakhon Si Thammarat on the west coast of the Gulf of Siam. Rather than take the long trail by land to the Central

Plate 2 — Sailing ship depicted on stone relief at Buddhist monument of
Borobudur, on Java (photo Wyatt 1991)

Plain of Siam, they probably yet again embarked by ship to a
port in the region of Ratchaburi. As late as the twelfth century,
what later became the Central Plain was still flooded, and they
probably continued by water up the Tha Chin River, perhaps
with an added cargo of dried fish or salt. By the time they
joined the Chaophraya River around Chainat they probably
transferred to smaller, rowed boats to continue up the Nan
River to Phitsanulok or up the Yom River to Sukhothai.

Chief among the commodities moving along these and other
trails in the twelfth century was Buddhism. It would be a
mistake, however, to think of this simply as the transfer of
religious ideas. In addition to religion, Buddhism also brought
with it the "latest" ideas of science, law, medicine, the letters,
and so forth; and these moved as quickly as they did because

they were coming into an area where Indic ideas were long established. For example, most of this region had devised its calendars and established its New Year (early, around the end of March by the Western calendar) using Indian methods that were much more accurate than the Western calendar until the shift was made from Julian to Gregorian reckoning in 1582.

Though by the 1180s King Jayavarman VII of Angkor might still be styled a *devaraja* and upheld a state religious system that centered on Shiva and Vishnu, and though at times he seemed to uphold Mahayana Buddhist deities, the Angkorean kings seriously underestimated the Theravada Buddhist belief and piety of increasing numbers of their subjects through much of what is now Thailand, Laos, and Cambodia. The most powerful of the ideas streaming into the region with Buddhism was a strict and persistent morality. Buddhism brought with it the idea that none but the moral and the holy might dare to touch—let alone to handle—the bodily relics of the Lord Buddha, such as a tooth or a fragment of bone (and the Buddha was thought to have been divided into 84,000 relics upon the end of his earthly existence).[1]

This was a period of rapid economic and social change. Long-lived power and prosperity had encouraged the growth and development of trading routes that criss-crossed mainland Southeast Asia and knit it to many of the lands and islands to the south and east. These especially connected the sources of numerous goods with the areas in which they were purchased, consumed, and used. These might have included the slaves, precious metals, and forest products of what is now southern

---

1. This idea is expanded at length in my "Relics, Oaths, and Politics in Thirteenth-Century Siam," *Journal of Southeast Asian Studies* 32:1 (February 2001), 3–66.

Laos; the luxury manufactured goods, including porcelain and damask, of what is now northern Vietnam; rarer metals common to (now) central Laos and the Phetchabun valley; the fine ceramics of the north; foodstuffs and tin from the Malay Peninsula; and so forth.

Many people were profiting from the surge in local and international trade. The most visible among these were the Chinese who may have run the north-south trade up and down the Tha Chin River, moving foodstuffs up the river and fine ceramics down it and abroad. Toward the end of this period they were moving to open a new overland trade to what was then southern Vietnam, over the mountains to Vinh via the middle Mekong. They were supported by the indigenous elite of the Yom and Nan River valleys, many of whom gained formal titles from the Angkorean kings, and even swore oaths in allegiance to them. Below them were the foremen who organized labor to fire the kilns and shape the pottery. All benefited from an inflow of labor from further north, in particular from the Kok River basin inland from Chiang Sæn and the upper Wang River basin of the Phayao and Phræ regions. The rich communities around them could afford the construction and maintenance of large, impressive religious buildings, which initially had been dedicated to the Hindu gods, but toward 1200 came to be Buddhist. Monks came to be trained, and embarked on pilgrimages to institutions of the middle peninsula and even to faraway Ceylon.

The young monks returned from their travels with heightened piety, with sprouts of the bodhi tree under which the Buddha had been enlightened, and even in a few rare cases with relics of the Buddha Himself. People soon came to know that only the most pious among men could dare even to touch the relics, lest they and their communities be afflicted with terrible ills. Shortly after the year 1200 there were several documented cases where ambitious rulers, confident of their high morality and buttressed by public approbation, dared to dig up or enshrine the relics.

There was much ferment in the region at the northern end of the Central Plain around 1220, and also in the far North (at Haripuñjaya), and there may also have been much at the head of the Gulf of Siam and in the region of Nakhon Si Thammarat. It may have been simultaneous by coincidence, or it may all have stemmed from similar developments. Our best guess would be that a flurry of activities involving Buddha relics (Haripuñjaya and Phræ around 1220) and the ceramics trade (the Ratchaburi region) and relations with Sri Lanka had common origins in a spurt in the international trade in ceramics which involved religious contacts across the Bay of Bengal. Ultimately the most important common thread that linked these developments was psychological and intellectual: rulers who embraced Theravâda Buddhism and at the same time built religious monuments involving bodily relics of the Lord Buddha were asserting their own self-confidence in their Buddhist morality, which soon would lead them to challenge the erstwhile rulers of the region in Angkor. In the short run, their self-confidence might have taken local expression, but by mid-century they were engaging and defeating Angkor's armies.

From perusing the written sources, whether stone inscriptions or Chinese records, you might never guess what was going through contemporary minds as the thirteenth century wore on. We do know enough, however, to be able to imagine what they might have been thinking. We know that this must have been an age that was in some ways quite frightening. The Mongols were in the process of conquering China, and soon moved to attack Vietnam and even to send a naval force against Java, as well as an invasion of inland Burma from Yunnan by the 1290s. Meanwhile, the kingdom of Angkor was issuing the last of its Sanskrit-language inscriptions and building among the last of its large stone monuments. To the ethnic and linguistic potpourri of central Indochina were added now many tens and even hundreds of thousands of Tai peoples, moving both southward from Yunnan and northern Laos, and southwestward from what is now northern Vietnam and adjacent portions of Laos.

What gave the Tai peoples some of their identity and self-confidence was their ability to handle the new economic production and marketing that surrounded (female-made) textiles and ceramics, and the experience that came from widespread (male) education and (male) participation in the life of the Buddhist monkhood. It was this self-confidence that, by the middle of the thirteenth century, gave them the self-confidence needed to challenge the Angkorean Empire and to win their independence. We don't know the dates when all this happened, but it probably included Sukhothai around 1247, Nakhon Si Thammarat by mid-century, Haripuñjaya by the 1270s, Chiang Mai and Chiang Sæn by the 1290s, and Nan sometime during this period. Luang Prabang and some places on the Khorat Plateau were to follow by the middle of the next century.

These "rebellions" are often referred to as the actions of the Tai or Thai; but were they really? Many of the places mentioned seem to have had populations that consisted of a variety of different ethnicities. In general, those towns east and south of a line stretching from Luang Prabang to Kanchanaburi were ethnically and linguistically more mixed than those places further north and west, and it would be legitimate to associate "rebellion" against Angkor with intellectual and economic considerations like religion and ceramics, rather than with ethnic and linguistic considerations.

Plate 3 — That Phanom monument. From book by the same name,
Bangkok: Muang Boran, n.d., frontispiece.

NAKHON  PHANOM

ALREADY WE HAVE ENCOUNTERED THE MEKONG
River valley several times in connection with the early history
of Siam, and we shall soon meet it again. But in treating the
early history of Siam, it is customary to find scant references to
the Mekong valley before the Bangkok period. What is the
point now of mentioning it earlier?

Though there are exceptions,[1] it is usual to include the northeastern part of Siam in the history of Laos until the French took
over Laos in 1893, and only to include it in Siam/Thailand after that date.[2] However, if we carefully consider the treatment
of the Khorat Plateau in this way, we might ask ourselves, Do
we really want so to privilege political history? Suddenly, overnight, at the stroke of a pen, does the northeastern part of what
is now Thailand cease being "part" of Laos and become thereafter a "part" of Thailand?

We might instead let a part of the world "declare" its
membership in one part of history or another by how it
behaves. In such terms, the middle Mekong valley in the early
centuries AD is a part of the history of Dvaravati; that is, that

---

1. Notably, for example, Hoshino Tatsuo, *Pour une histoire medievale du
Moyen Mekong* (Bangkok: Editions Duang Kamol, 1986).

2. For example, see Martin Stuart-Fox, *The Lao Kingdom of Lan Xang:
Rise and Decline* (Bangkok: White Lotus, 1998).

slice of territory stretching from the head of the Gulf of Siam to the middle of the Gulf of Tonkin. I am thinking in particular of that part of the region we already have met and will meet again, stretching back from the Mekong River and the That Phanom monument toward Sakon Nakhon, Kalasin, and the upper basin of the Chi River, as well as the basin of the small Songkhram River. Technically, this is the northeastern part of the Northeast.[3]

There is no better way for the region to define its own history than for us to look at the physical and written remains it has left us. First, we can hardly miss the towering monument known as That Phanom, now located just to the south of Nakhon Phanom. It was reconstructed after collapsing in August 1975. Its date is uncertain, but we can be fairly sure that there was some monument constructed there toward the middle of the first millennium AD. We know that it continued to be a focus of local life almost continuously since then, right to the present day.

Next we might consider the unusual remains of Müang Fa Dæt in what is now Kalasin province. It clearly dates from the sixth to the ninth centuries of the current era, and has certain affinities with Angkor, as we saw in chapter 2.

The third set of historical data with which we can begin comes from the Vietnamese annals written in the fourteenth century which tell us that Siam contacted Vietnam early in the fourteenth century. It seems reasonably certain that the contact was made over the Mu Gia Pass in 1318.[4] The Mu Gia Pass is

3. The reader will find extremely useful Srisakara Vallibhotama, *A Northeastern Site of Civilization: New Archaeological Evidence to Change the Face of Thai History* (Bangkok: Sinlapa Watthanatham, 1990), which includes English summaries for each chapter.

4. Georges Maspero, *Le royaume de Champa* (Paris: van Oest, 1928), pp. 196–7, fn. 5.

directly east (by about 100 kilometers/60 miles) from Nakhon Phanom.

A fourth bit of evidence comes from an inscription in Sukhothai language and Sukhothai script from Sakon Nakhon (75 kilometers/50 miles west of Nakhon Phanom) dated in early 1351.

If we take these four references together and imagine that they work together to draw arrows across the landscape, we might then ask where are those arrows pointing? The answer is that they are pointing generally to the northeast and to the southwest. They do not seem to be pointing either to the north or northwest (toward Vientiane) or to the south (toward Angkor and Cambodia).

What follows has to do with the "why" question of what reasons there might have been for the people in Nakhon Phanom to be so oriented in a northeasterly and southwesterly direction. Why might they have been so oriented?

The southwest "arrow" is fairly straightforward. It was from the southwest that India came to the Nakhon Phanom region. That is, from the southwest came Buddhism and Indian arts and sciences. But how did they come? There were no electronic media then. If texts and ideas were coming, they were transported by people. The distances were sufficiently long, and the rigors of travel were so heavy, that we might imagine that few travelers might have been inspired to make the journey for ideas and beliefs alone. No, (and this is a twentieth or twenty-first century prejudice) it is likely that travelers were encouraged to travel by economic motivations.

The best guess might be that the Nakhon Phanom (or That Phanom) area was the ideal link between the Mu Gia Pass over the mountains to the coasts of Vietnam and Champa, and their large populations, and the areas of the Khorat Plateau which produced pottery and agricultural products. There must have been considerable income here from the distance trade, and from a large inland market, for a great deal seems to have been spent in That Phanom and its vicinity. Nakhon Phanom was to continue to be a major center through the eighteenth century.

AYUTTHAYA AND ITS NEIGHBORS, 1351

ON 4 MARCH 1351, A SMALL GROUP OF MEN gathered
in a newly built hall on an island in the Chaophraya River.
Before them was an urn filled with water gathered from
throughout Siam, stirred with a magical sword, and which they
drank swearing their loyalty to the relative who was becoming
their king (soon remembered as Ramathibodi I). The capital of
a new kingdom there was taking shape.[1]

What happened that day (and we still lack any reliable
accounts) has much to tell us about the processes that were then
at work. First, many of the people then present were related to
the new king, and soon would govern many of the surrounding
towns and their territory. Many of them were native speakers
of the Cambodian language (Khmer); and all the high-ranking
among them possessed gold or copper plates on which were
inscribed their formal titles. Much of the oath which they

---

1. Thai schoolbooks and scholars cling tenaciously to the idea that
Ayudhya was founded in 1350, having long ago been told that Lesser Era
(*chulasakkarat*) years are converted to AD years by adding 638. The reason
for the discrepancy is simple: the year 712 began on the 7th day of the
waning moon of the 5th month, and continued until 713 began on the 1st
day of the 6th month in the next year (365 days later), the interval being
from 28 March 1350 to 28 March 1351. Thus the 6th day of the waxing
moon of the 5th month did not occur until 4 March 1351 (Julian calendar).

Plate 4 — Foundation of Ayutthaya, 1351. From *Siam: General and Medical Features* (Bangkok, 1930), opp. p. 140.

swore was like the oaths taken by colleagues even to the present day; but there was another part that is almost unintelligible nowadays. It was that part of the oath that warned men that the spirits of particular named streams and caves would punish them if they failed to keep their promise of loyalty.[2] It is fascinating to note that those spirits were localized in extreme northern Thailand and adjacent portions of Laos. Either the spirits were being imported (which is unlikely), or the animistic

2. Text of the oath is given in Plüang na Nakhòn, *Prawat Wannakhadi Thai samrap naksüksa* (6th ed.; Bangkok, 1967), pp. 42–47. See also *Photcananukrom sap wannakhadi Thai samai Ayutthaya Lilit ongkan chæng nam* (Bangkok, 1997). The best analysis of the oath is in Cit Phumisak, *Ongkan chæng nam* (2nd ed.; Bangkok, 1981).

See also my "Three Sukhothai Oaths of Allegiance," in Wyatt, *Studies in Thai History* (Chiang Mai: Silkworm Books, 1996), 59–68.

22

religion employed here was rooted in the north, from whence some of these people came.

But who were these people, and why were they here? The best guess is that those functioning as scribes, lawyers, accountants, chronologists, astrologers, and similar specialists probably were persons associated with "East Siam"—i.e., Lopburi, Nakhon Nayok, and similar old localities once part of the Angkorean Empire. On the other hand, the administrative and military functionaries probably were people from "West Siam"— especially Suphanburi, Ratchaburi, and Phetchaburi, for example. Lurking in the shadows there may have been an important third group of people—Chinese and Indian merchants. About them we know very little, except that they were intimately involved in the trade of Siam by the early fourteenth century. One of their many interests was the ceramics trade, which earlier had brought them to the valley of the Tha Chin River, especially to Ratchaburi and Suphanburi.

The one person who tied together all these groups was the new king, Ramathibodi I (also referred to as U Thong). Our best guess is that his wife was the daughter of the late king of Suphanburi, while his mother was the daughter of the ruler of Lopburi and his father was a Chinese merchant of Phetchaburi. It is important to note that he brought all three of these groups together, and from each of these he gained important resources. With his Lopburi relatives he gained many generations of expertise in rulership, including skills in such things as law and medicine. His Suphanburi relatives brought with them manpower and military skills, while his Phetchaburi relatives gave him skills with such things as commerce and cash. The combination would have been hard to equal.

It has been conventional to treat the early history of Ayutthaya (Siam) in terms of its foreign policy, and thus to focus particularly upon Ayutthaya's continuing rivalry with neighboring Angkor, which after all was only 250 miles/400 kilometers to its east. We might note particularly Ayutthaya's capture of Angkor in 1369 and again in 1431. Here we might imagine that Ramathibodi was acting on behalf of his Lopburi relatives, who might be expected to see Angkor as their chief rival for prestige and power. But rather than defining their interests as being relatively more universalistic or "global," perhaps we might instead see their interest as being more local than the interests of Suphanburi.

Suphanburi, after all, in addition to aspiring to leadership of all the areas to the west of Lopburi, including both the north and the south, might be expected to have not only a strong interest in the ceramics trade—which would reach its peak by the late fifteenth century—but also to have had a strong interest in the trade which extended not only to the center and south of what is now Laos and adjacent Vietnam, but also over the trade routes which extended to the west and south across the Malay Peninsula and into the Bay of Bengal.

It is in this context that we might interpret a stone inscription which otherwise is quite puzzling. This is a stone dated to 17 February 1351 and to the Reliquary of Ban Ræ in what is now Sakon Nakhon province.[3] This is what amounts to a Sukhothai inscription. Why is it here? The only way to account for it is to link it with Vietnamese literary references dated to 1318 to a Sukhothai intrusion into Champa in central Vietnam.[4] But what is Sukhothai doing all the way east in central Vietnam? The only way of accounting for this is to explore economic

---

3. Thawat Punnothok, *Sila carük Isan samai Thai-Lao* (Bangkok: Ramkhamhæng University, 1987), pp. 225–227.

4. Georges Maspero, *Le royaume de Champa* (Paris: van Oest, 1928), pp. 196–7, fn. 5.

considerations; and if the Ban Ræ inscription leads us from Sukhothai to the east, then it would seem natural to look southwards from Sukhothai as well.

In conceptualizing this early period of Siam's history, it is customary to think of it first in terms of religion. Early stone inscriptions detailing the history of Buddhism, for example, often refer to Buddhist monks as *chao thai*, that is, "Thai lords." It is worth remembering, however, the emphasis that the Ramkhamhæng inscription of 1292 places upon economic policy, on the freedom of buying and selling, and on the lightness of taxation. This leads us back to reconsidering the important role of economic activity in the foundation of Ayutthaya and in the location of the Sakon Nakhon inscription, both in early 1351.

Here we might begin with a simple point. Let us simply note that the earliest contemporary reference to the foundation of Ayutthaya occurs two years before it was formally founded in 1351, when Chinese merchants reported in 1349 that Ayutthaya had been created, *and* that it was now named with a Persian or Arabic name that we might translate as "New City" (Shahr i-Naw), implying that an "Old City" had preceded it. By the later years of the century, a mission from Suphanburi was seeking in China the right to trade as a tributary mission. A bit later, in 1416, the Ayutthaya court was persuaded to double the customs duties charged.[5] Finally, shortly after the catastrophic events in 1424 which ended the lives of two candidates (Ai Phraya and Yi Phraya) for the throne of the

5. Ishii Yoneo, "The *Rekidai Hôan* and Some Aspects of the Ayutthayan Port Polity in the Fifteenth Century," *Memoirs of the Toyo Bunko 50* (1992), 81–92; also his "Some aspects of the 15th century Ayutthayan port-polity as seen from a Ryukyuan source," *South East Asian Research* 2:1 (March 1994), 53–64.

Plate 5 — Chao Ai Phraya and Chao Yi Phraya duel on elephant-back.
From *Khlong phap phraratchaphongsawadan* (Bangkok: Birthday of
Princess Galyani, 1983), p. 8.

kingdom of Ayutthaya, a major religious monument was
constructed in their memory in the city (Wat Ratchaburana),
and inscriptions were left inside it written in Thai, Khmer,
Chinese, and Arabic.[6] These were not discovered until the
1950s, so we can be confident of their authenticity. Their
significance is ritualistic: that is, in a monument of the greatest
importance, at least these four languages were considered to be
relevant to memorializing the early kings of Ayutthaya. Even
in the style of the early fifteenth century, Ayutthaya was
expressing its true globalization.

6. *Citrakam læ sinlapawatthu nai kru phraprang Wat Ratchaburana*
(Bangkok: Fine Arts Dept., 1959); and *Phraphuttharup læ phraphim nai
phraprang Wat Ratchaburana* (Bangkok: Fine Arts Dept., 1959).

MEN  AT WAR

WHEN DISCUSSING WARFARE, IT IS CUSTOMARY
to speak of warriors as men. It is probable that most warriors
indeed were men, but it was not unheard of for women to fight
at their sides But let us begin by referring to warriors as
(mostly) men, who may on occasion have been joined by
women. Remember that women figured prominently in premodern battles at Phuket (Thalang) and Khorat (Nakhon
Ratchasima), and probably at many other places. And let us
begin by noting that, when the call went out for warriors to
assemble and join an army to be sent against Cambodia, the
Lao, or the Burmese, it was probably mostly younger men who
gathered up their weapons, food, and spare clothing, and
donned their white cotton underjackets that conferred
invulnerability on them.[1]

Relatively small armies, numbering in the tens of thousands,
might have assembled in the fourteenth, fifteenth, and
sixteenth centuries. Of these, probably a few dozen men were
mounted on elephants, for which they would have had some
prior training or experience. Of the three men atop an

---

1. I have never forgotten the slide shown (where? time?) by Baas Terwiel,
showing little cotton jackets in Buddhist, Muslim, and Christian contexts
in Southeast Asia.

elephant, the person in the middle might have been a high-ranking prince or high official, while the person ahead of him directed and "steered" the elephant and the person just above the beast's tail guarded against attacks from the rear. Probably the person in the middle wielded a long-handled spear or war-scythe; but the most critical "weapon" might have been the elephant's tusks, which might have been piloted against opposing creatures' eyes and tusks.

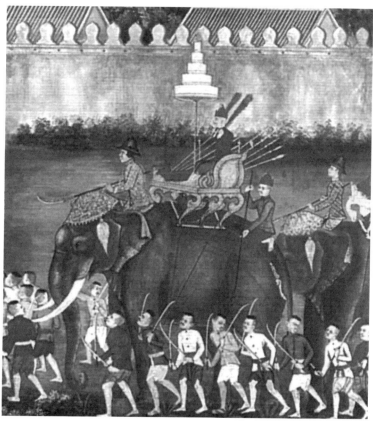

Plate 6 — Detail of an elephant at war. From *Khlong phap phraratcha-phongsawadan* (Bangkok: Birthday of Princess Galyani, 1983), p. 50.

The elephants we can see in the circus or the zoo seem to be relatively docile creatures, and not very warlike. They probably were not fierce, and had to be prepared for battle, as in this passage which probably derives from firsthand experience from a time (1827) when elephants still were used in battle:

Mün Mòk Lòng [of] Phayao stopped to rest and eat [breakfast] beside the road. Mün Kæo Nakhòn caught up with him, and asked, "Whose army is ahead of me here?" He was told, "The force of the governor of Phayao." Mün Kæo Nakhòn asked, "Why aren't you fighting? Why are you stopped? You're shirking your duty! I'm going to fight the king of the South." Mün Mòk Lòng of Phayao said, "As for me, I have gained [by fighting] many towns and villages for the king— I don't know how many. I'm no child. Don't impugn my bravery."

Then [Mün Mòk Lòng] gave three pots of tonic herbs to his elephant, Meng Garuda, to consume.[2] Then he mounted his elephant, asked for his goad, and signaled him to go and fight the elephant of the governor of Chaliang-Sukhothai, named Klamphæng-phekphon. Mün Mòk Lòng fought him to the peak of Dòi Pa Kò protecting against Meng Garuda's tusks breaking; and although Meng Garuda's tusk was broken off, he defeated the elephant of the Southerner. Ten elephants of the Southerners fell from the mountain top and died.[3]

Language experts say that the "tonic herbs" mentioned are probably some sort of amphetamines.

We might smile here at the good-natured banter between the two warriors meeting on the road to battle!

2. We have not seen such a reference before—elephants being given (presumably) stimulants before a battle.

3. David K. Wyatt and Aroonrut Wichienkeeo, *The Chiang Mai Chronicle* (2nd ed., Chiang Mai, 1998), pp. 82–83. This is within a decade of the war recorded in the next passage.

Combat on elephant-back might have been rather fearsome, as we can tell from this passage in the Chronicle of the Principality of Nan, referring to warfare early in the fifteenth century:

He had ruled for one year when, in the *ka pao* year, CS 797,[4] Cao Intakæn obtained troops from the ruler of Chaliang and led them [towards Nan], setting up his base at the mouth of the Samun [river], north of Cæ Pang. Cao Pæng brought down an army to engage the invaders, mounted on his war elephant, Prap Cakravala, and crossed the river north of the mouth of the Samun. Intakæn, mounted on his war elephant, Khwan Phek Paña Mara, charged the elephant Prap Cakravala. Khwan Phek engaged [his adversary], and was struck right at the end of his tusk(s). Khwan Phek was wounded by the tusk of Prap Cakravala.

Prap Cakravala then withdrew back across the Nan River [and got set in a position] using the Nan and Samun rivers as moats, [along which] the army assembled. Cao Pæng decided to fight [Intakæn] there. Cao Intakæn, mounted on Khwan Phek Paña Mara, crossed the Nan River [in pursuit]. Tao Pæng, heedless of his elephant's royally-decorated tusks, engaged Tao Intakæn's elephant Khwan Phek, and the tips of [Prap Cakravala's] tusks stabbed into the mouth of his opponent, and the latter lost all taste for battle. Then Intakæn slashed with his lance, and Cao Pæng, bleeding profusely, fell from his elephant and died.

Intakæn's troops then made short work of their opponents, killing them and driving them into the Samun to drown. The place where the two princes dueled on the Samun north of Cæ Pang, where Cao Pæng was killed, is popularly known as the Na Khacat ["Massacre

4. Probably CS 796 (AD 1434).

Plate 7 — King Intharacha battles Mün Nakhòn, from a painting by Luang Suwannasit. From *Khlong phap phraratchaphongsawadan* (1983), p. 10.

Field"]; and the place where their armies battled is called Ban Khwai Mæng Ngang; ["Village of the Rout"]. Cao Pæng died in the *ka pao* year, CS 797.[5]

It is hard to know what the weaponry of these soldiers was. We might expect some warriors used swords and crossbows. Later, a few might have been armed with firearms of some sort,

5. David K. Wyatt, *The Nan Chronicle* (Ithaca, 1994), pp. 51–52.

31

from arquebuses to matchlocks. Early references to firearms are probably mistranslations, but at some early point there may have been some kinds of cannon present, from perhaps early in the seventeenth century. But the early weaponry was probably predominantly composed of knives and swords, supplemented by sharpened farm implements and bamboo. Some accounts even mention a kind of bungee-pit—a deep pit with sharpened bamboo sticks at the bottom, and the whole pit covered with cloth and false earth, with leaves and small shrubs atop that. Attackers would be directed toward the pit, into which they would fall and be impaled.

One account, probably taken from an indigenous account of the wars between the Chinese (Hò) and the Tai Yuan of the Chiang Mai region tell us how the Yuan soldiers overcame the shock of first encountering soldiers with armor, which resisted the weapons directed against them.

All the Hò wore iron and copper and leather armor. Our men went out to capture Hò, and [brought back] one man, whom they asked, "Why don't you die when hit, slashed, shot with spears and swords and guns and arrows? How can we defeat you?" [The man replied,] "Use hot sand and pebbles hurled with iron ladles down their necklines in order to roast and burn them, and then they'll be defeated."

So advised, our men swept up sand and pebbles to be heated as red-hot as fire, and [gathered] iron ladles to hurl them; and they heated them over fire. The Hò were defeated, and retreated back to their own country.[6]

6. Wyatt and Aroonrut, *The Chiang Mai Chronicle*, p. 76.

Some of the encounters between local soldiers and invading Khmer, Lao, Burmese, and others may have been fought with weapons no more threatening than fists and feet, and indeed much of the local martial arts tradition may have its origins in premodern warfare. But the point of this whole discussion is to argue that whether with elephants, or armor, there was much in the actions of early peasants that has to be thought of in terms of creative thinking.

ANGKOR AND SUKHOTHAI, 1430–1450

THE CHRONICLES OF AYUTTHAYA TELL US THAT in 1431 the Ayutthaya king took Angkor and established his son to rule there. We are given no details about the background to this event, and are left only to imagine the long-standing conflicts that might lie behind it. We are, however, told that the Ayutthaya people gathered up a variety of images. The chronicles say simply that

> The King then had Phraya Kæo, Phraya Thai, and their families, as well as all the images of sacred oxen and all the images of lions and other creatures, brought along. When they reached Ayutthaya, the King therefore had all of the animal images taken and presented as offerings, some at the Phra Si Ratana Maha That Monastery and some at the Phra Si Sanphet Monastery.[1]

We are never told what these images might have been.

If we follow up on the earlier economic references, including the various inscriptions from Wat Ratchaburana, we might

---

1. *The Royal Chronicles of Ayutthaya*, tr. Richard D. Cushman, ed. David K. Wyatt (Bangkok: Siam Society, 2000), p. 15, lines 31–39. I continue to have doubts about this translation. The initial reference to the "Phraya Kæo" and "Phraya Thai" may simply be a reference to petty rulers of Vietnamese and Thai ethnicity.

imagine that the invasion of Angkor gave Ayutthaya control over the various trade routes to the southeast, toward Chanthaburi, and also to the northeast, toward Nakhon Ratchasima (Khorat) and the basin of the Mun River.

This economic interpretation of the capture of Angkor does not, however, satisfy the questions of the context in which it is set. Consider that the various chronicles continue on to follow the conquest of Angkor with another set of important conquests, notably the capture of Sukhothai in 1438 and attacks against Chiang Mai shortly thereafter.

What made warfare work, of course, was manpower. Armies needed lots of manpower in order to work, particularly as more elephants and horses were employed and had to be fed and cared for.

At the same time, the reward of successful warfare was additional captured manpower. The usual tactic was for the Ayutthaya kings to site captured manpower on the opposite side of the capital from where they had been captured. Thus, men taken in the north were sent to live in the south, and men captured in the east were sent to live in the west. That is why those captured in the Sukhothai region in the fifteenth century were sent to live in the extreme south. It is said that, today, those speaking the most archaic dialect of Sukhothai Thai are now found in the modern province of Narathiwat, on the border with Kelantan; Lao are especially concentrated in Kanchanaburi province, and those speaking dialects closely related to Khmer are to be found in the modern province of Suphanburi.[2]

2. See J. Marvin Brown, *From Ancient Thai to Modern Dialects* (Bangkok: White Lotus, 1985).

Around the middle of the sixteenth century, there was constant warfare both east and north of Ayutthaya. As troops frequently were being captured and resettled, the populations in the kingdom of Ayutthaya were growing, and their administrations frequently were being renovated. Although a population increment was especially composed of Tai-speaking peoples, there were also many others of different ethnic, cultural, and linguistic backgrounds. Certainly as late as the fifteenth century, and surely later as well, there was such ethnic variety in the population as to require that public documents, like letters of appointment, had to be written in at least two languages, including especially Khmer in the Central Plain and in the South.

It was during the reign of King Trailok (1448–88) that major renovations are thought to have been made in the administration. The *Royal Chronicles* attach two changes to the administration: the old simple Thai terms for the major departments of state were changed to Sanskrit names and titles, and all the ranks were associated with numerical rankings. The first indicates that the administrative organization was cast anew in an Indic mode derived perhaps from the Angkorean administration.

Both Trailok's reforms worked to facilitate the creation of a more layered society. In addition to dividing the civilian from the military wings of government, the revised administration allowed for a more intricate layering of major and minor government organs (ministries, departments, bureaus, etc.). Similarly, the assignment of numerical ranks to everyone ranged all people in a single hierarchy. At the bottom of the ladder were slaves and women, at a rank of just 10, while male commoners ranked 25. Lower-ranking officials might rank between 40 and 400, while higher officials ranked from a low

of 400 to a ministry head at as much as 10,000. Members of
the royal family straddled that figure, while the king alone
enjoyed a rank of infinity. All of this meant that there were
literally hundreds of possible ranks, which confirmed the
popular view that everyone was higher or lower than someone
else, which might find common expression in dress, behavior,
and even physical altitude: high-ranking people might stand in
the presence of almost all others (except the king), while low-
ranking persons crouched or crawled in the presence of others.
This sense of higher and lower rank was expressed in the
gestures made by all, with the two hands joined together and
raised higher or lower depending on the relative rank
differential between two individuals meeting each other.

Above, reference was made to "slaves." In early centuries,
slaves were probably recruited and captured from people
thought of as "uncivilized." They were referred to as *khròk*, a
word otherwise reserved for creatures that were born in litters,
like dogs and cats. They might have originated as true chattel
property, as little more than savages taken from people up in
the hills, a phenomenon which we know was common in
mediaeval Angkor. By the fourteenth and fifteenth centuries,
these would especially have included war captives. Soon it
became possible for them to gain their independence (and
eligibility for military service) by cash payments or the
benevolence of their "owners." There soon developed (as
shown by M.R. Akin Rabibhadana) a tension between slaves
who were the "property" of individuals, and others who by
monetary debt became the "debt slaves" of powerful figures,
and, on the other hand, those who were attached for labor
service to "the king" or "the government." Akin argues that
dynasties often began by registering all "slaves" and "freemen"
as the property of the government, succeeded by periods when

37

more and more people enlisted as the slaves of others, in order to evade compulsory government labor service, or to raise cash for some family emergency (like, for example, a daughter's wedding). Perhaps the point of all this is that although the social structure was rigid and well-ordered, it was also sufficiently flexible to allow for the movement of individuals and groups in order to improve their situation.

It is difficult to attribute the creation of this social and administrative structure to any specific or named individual. In the same fashion it is rare that we know the names of any who created the masterpieces of early Thai literature or wrote the early treatises on warfare or Buddhist religious thought. Things tend to be attributed to the kings in whose reigns these were written, but this must not be interpreted as "attribution" in the Western sense. This is analogous to the way in which the political chaos that marred the late 1540s is usually blamed on a love match between two individuals. In truth, however, surely many others were involved. We might be left with the simpler assertion that royal power had now become worth fighting over.

FAMILPOLITICS

KING NARESUAN (R. 1590–1605) AND THE BROTHER
who succeeded him, King Ekathotsarot (r. 1605–1610) had
seen their polity through a long period of turbulence after the
Burma armies had sacked Ayutthaya and many of its neighbors
in the 1560s, 1570s, and 1580s. In addition to fighting the
armies from the other side of the mountains, and trying to
rebuild the kingdom's military strength, the brothers had been
trying to reorganize the administration, which had been
devastated by four decades of war. Not only did they need new
revenues for the necessary self-strengthening, it was now clear
that they needed new resources with which to buy the newer
military technology which had been utilized in the recent wars
and hire the mercenary specialists now necessary.

Not surprisingly, the central administration now moved to
strengthen its overseas trade, and used that trade to bolster its
defenses. The provincial administration was expanded to give
the Kalahom Ministry greater access to the wealth of the
southern provinces, and an expanded role in the military
preparedness of the kingdom.

In this context, we also must not forget that the Portuguese
had been around for nearly a century, and the Spaniards were
well established in the Philippines. As if that were not enough,
the Chinese, Japanese, Ryukyuans, and even Koreans were

more active in the region than they had been before, and perhaps there was more seaborne trade from the South Asian subcontinent than there had been for a long time before. Moreover, we are on the verge of seeing a dramatic increase in commerce with other Europeans, with the Dutch and English newly arrived on the scene and other Europeans soon to follow.

It was in this context that, in 1605, at the end of Naresuan's reign or the beginning of Ekathotsarot's, that a pair of traders arrived from the Persian Gulf region. We don't know what kind of ship they came on—Indian or Arab—nor are we positive where they came from or what they were doing. Their descendants believe that they came from the island of Kuni, where both Arabic and Persian are spoken. The elder, a man known as Sheik Ahmad, was unmarried, and soon took a Thai wife and left his Islamic religion, while the other, Mohammed Said, remained a Muslim and presumably took a Muslim wife. Either they came with a lot of commercial expertise or they had a great deal of natural talent. Because they were quickly put to work on government organs dealing with overseas trade, there is good reason to believe that their language skills were important to the Siamese. These were not entirely new— remember the Arabic-language inscription of 1424—and we might be encouraged to think that Indian Ocean trade with Indians and Arabs was increasing.

We are told that Sheik Ahmad soon became the Minister of Interior, a cabinet-level position. Why the Ministry of Interior (Mahatthai)? We tend to think of this as a government administrative organ oriented toward the North and Northeast; but we need to remember that Indian Ocean trade tended to focus on the Gulf of Martaban coast and the Tenasserim region, which were more closely associated with the Mahatthai. It is even possible that the administration was attempting to use the Mahatthai to balance the increased weight of the Phrakhlang and Kalahom, who were the chief beneficiaries of South China Sea and Gulf of Siam trade.

The seventeenth century must have been a treacherous time, politically. There was a good deal of movement into and out of the ministerial positions, and the political in-fighting must have been severe. Sheik Ahmad, however, seems to have held his position, and he had only recently been in power when a diplomatic mission came to Siam from the king of Persia in 1685–86.[1] The Persian envoy gives us the impression that Sheik Ahmad had fortunate relations with the Persian trading community, and that the latter were well ensconced in the western part of the kingdom, as well as in the capital.

What was beginning here in the seventeenth century was a close relationship between Siam's administration and members of the family descended from Sheik Ahmad, referred to as the Bunnag family. They continue to be prominent especially in the conduct of Thailand's foreign policy, as well as in various branches of the government.

1. John O'Kane, tr., *The Ship of Sulaiman* (London: Routledge & Kegan Paul, 1972). See also my "Family Politics in Seventeenth- and Eighteenth-Century Siam," *Studies in Thai History* (Chiang Mai: Silkworm Books, 1996), 97–105.

SUN AND PLANETS, SONS AND PLANTS

THERE IS A FILIPINO FOLK SONG WHICH BEGINS by telling us what all Southeast Asian farmers already know: "Planting rice is never fun. Work from dawn to the set of sun." But people have done it for a long time, because rice is a very efficient crop. Its nutritional density is very high, that is, the farmer gets a lot of calories for each unit of land; and rice responds well to labor inputs. When the family is large and requires a lot of food, then more rice can be grown on the same land with the addition of the labor of the children. When the children have left home, then the old folks can still eat well with the rice grown on the land remaining, and even earn money from renting out their unused land.

Rice also depends on reliable water supply on level land. There is a long dry period each year, followed by the onset of monsoon rains around about the same week each year. The rains continue in great quantity for four or five months, and then end at about the time when the rice has grown and needs to dry and be harvested. For Siam, the first critical period comes in June or July, when seedlings sprout and grow thickly to the point when they are readied for transplanting.

All depends, then, on the careful and accurate measurement of time. There is no snow to watch melt, and no temperatures to begin rising. The farmer has to know when it is June, or time to plant. He or she has to know when to expect the rains. We might expect that the moon would provide a reliable time measurement, figuring that the lunar month lasts about thirty days. The trouble is, that the lunar year lasts for 354 days. Since the "real," solar year lasts for 365.25 days, the lunar year causes the farmer to "speed up" more than eleven days each year, so a new lunar year comes every 354 days. It took farmers and statesmen in the West a long time to measure annual time exactly, so it was not until 1582 (1752 in Britain and North America) that the exact length of the year could be settled on. Some religious holidays, East and West, which depend on combinations of lunar and solar time, are enormously complicated—note the Easter tables in many Christian prayer handbooks, for example.

Fortunately, the Indo-European farmers in India worked out the calendar problem very early, and from there the calendar was exported to Southeast Asia by about the seventh century. We don't know exactly when it came, or when it was adapted to local latitudes, but Chris Eade figures that it was about AD 638 in a locality for Siam around present-day Lopburi. There are numerous examples of the calendar being inscribed on stone from the seventh century or so.

The calendar yields a long list of numbers, giving us, for example, the exact moment when the year began, the exact position in the skies of the sun, moon, and all the planets, and many other numbers. We might think that the calendar was based upon observation—that is, noting where in the skies various heavenly bodies were, using something like the same devices as our astrological signs (Virgo, Aquarius, and so forth). But there are numerous examples of correct planetary positions given, for example, which were patently not observable. No, calendars were worked out by calculation. There are numerous cases where we have examples of the calculations, either incised on stone or written on indigenous paper.

The calculations that produced a calendar were (and are) enormously complex. These included very sophisticated mathematical operations, such as dividing a three- or four-digit number into a six-digit number, and using the remainder of the division-operation in the next stage of operations. (I used to do such operations by pencil on paper, in the years before electronic calculators, and I could only do the calculations for two years in one day of work.)

Farmers were not the only persons who required an accurate signal for the beginning of the year. Courts and other rulers wanted calendrical guidance to establish the ceremonies with which the year began. We used to assume that the calculations were too complicated and too difficult to be left to poor, uneducated, "peasants." But that is a condescension! Besides, where might experts and other technicians have come from? No, there was a lot of such numerical and calendrical sophistication "out there" in the countryside. Of that, there is quite a bit of evidence, including a lot of what is equivalent to "scratch-pads."

We all know a lot of people who were or are mathematical geniuses, or experts; or people capable of understanding and visualizing and explaining very complex matters. Probably most villages had several such people (including both men and women). Someone "out there" could be gone to for advice on when to plant the rice or when to expect the monsoon rains. Sometimes such "experts" were wrong, as the chronologists were in Ayutthaya for a while in the eighteenth century. Once in a while a copyist might copy an astronomical diagram upside-down, but such occurrences were rare.

And so, when the French intellectual Simon de La Loubère went to Siam in the 1680s, he found a high standard of astronomical science, astrology, and even mathematics.[1] This was not a society of illiterate, uneducated dolts, but a society in which there was considerable scientific and mathematical sophistication.

Someone in Ayutthaya times would have been able to read something like the following diagram, which tells us of the disposition of the heavenly bodies on 30 June, AD 2001:

> On that day, Venus and Saturn were in Taurus; the Sun, Mercury, Jupiter, and Rahu in Gemini, the Moon in Libra, and Mars in Scorpio. In that year, CS 1263, the year began on the 8th day of the waning half of the fifth moon, and the day was a Saturday, the 10th day of the waxing half of the eighth moon.[2]

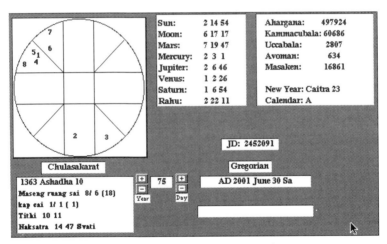

Plate 8 — Planetary configuration for 30 June 2001

1. Simon de La Loubère, *The Kingdom of Siam* (Kuala Lumpur: Oxford University Press, 1969), II, 168–169.

2. My reading of the data provided by the program of Lars Gislén and Chris Eade, "SEAsian Calendars v. 3.7.7," computer program for Apple Macintosh.

BOROMMAKOT AND CHINESE

PROBABLY MANY RULERS OF OLD SIAM ARE
known by nicknames or other epithets, but one of the most
striking is King Borommakot (1733–58), whose common
name is the "golden urn" in which he reposed awaiting
cremation. He is often thought of as having presided over an
age that was golden, like the urn in which he "sat" for many
months; but he might better be thought of as lending his name
to a majestic urban transformation.

In the seventeenth century, Chinese trade, particularly with
the Philippines, brought enormous quantities of (especially
Mexican) silver to China, which during that century brought
considerable prosperity that was noticeable in the cities of
China. By the early eighteenth century, however, that silver
began to flow abroad in ever-increasing qualities. What drew it
abroad was the need to feed a rapidly increasing population.
Inhibited for a time by punitive Chinese legislation, the
Chinese search abroad for additional foodstuffs accelerated
after an imperial decree in 1722 explicitly mentioning the
exchange of silver for Siamese rice:

> The Hsien-lo [Siamese] people say that rice is plentiful in their land
> and two or three ounces of silver can buy one picul [133.33 lbs.] of
> paddy. We have given orders to have rice transported to Fukien

[southeast China] and other places. It would be very beneficial to those places.[1]

The Chinese probably learned as quickly as the Dutch and English had, that they had no desire to drain their country of bullion in order to buy food. They had to pay for those imports either with exports (porcelain, brocade, tea) or by profits gained in trade within the rest of Asia.

It just happened that, at about the same time, disposable incomes within Southeast Asia were benefiting from a new surge in exports to Europe. In particular, tea and coffee were being shipped from Java and coastal China, pepper was being shipped from numerous ports of Southeast Asia, and hemp was in high demand from the Philippines to rig sailing ships. It required only new entrepreneurial energies to stimulate the export of sugar and aromatic woods, as well as rice, from Siam. Even internal markets within Siam might profit from such energies applied to gambling and the production of fruits.

Not only did the ethnic Chinese population of Siam rapidly increase, but it was especially concentrated in Ayutthaya and in the provinces around the head of the Gulf of Siam. The population was most concentrated there, and so were the money and the power. Just as a century or two later, Chinese populations tended to cluster around transportation routes (first canals and trails, later railroads). Siam was in dire need of a labor supply, since Siamese labor was occupied for four to six months a year with compulsory labor service for the government, or indentured labor for slaveholders or officials. We might expect, then, for Chinese labor to be clustered in

1. G. William Skinner, *Chinese Society in Thailand* (Ithaca: Cornell University Press, 1957), p. 17.

places where their labor was most needed. Indeed, Chinese were concentrated in the southeastern part of the island of Ayutthaya, where seagoing ships landed when first arriving. There they might expect to find employment as stevedores, and also in packing and storing goods, both imported and exported. But many Chinese came also to be employed in accounting and in commercial correspondence.

Many observers have remarked that the numerous Siamese government ships sent both by offices and by officials were manned by Chinese sailors and officers. It is likely that many others were employed at the Siam end of the trade as specialists working, for example, to sort the valuable from the worthless commodities, the edible from the inedible birds'-nests and so forth. Still others might have assumed the tasks of organizing and ruling the resident Chinese community. The most prosperous among them might have bid or bribed their way into organizing tax collection, or lotteries and gambling, or even tax collection. We tend to imagine the resident Chinese community as being lower class, composed of laborers and petty entrepreneurs. It is important to remind ourselves that there was a significant middle- and upper-class element among them.

It is this variegated quality of the resident Chinese that helps us account for the presence and vitality of an element in the population of the city that might otherwise be forgotten. I am thinking here of a well-organized sector of the Chinese population that specialized in public entertainment. Here were boxers, ærialists, actors, acrobats, magicians, and prostitutes, among many others. These were drawn by an anonymous artist later in the century, who seems to have regarded them as an established part of the life of the capital.

And of course not all the Chinese were male. Even if most

Plate 9 — Acrobats from a temple fair in the 1770s.
From *Prachum mai rap sang* (Bangkok, 1980).

immigrants from China were men, many subsequently married local women and had children, half of whom were female. We know of at least three persons who were born to mixed Sino-Siamese couples, all of them born around 1740; and surely there were many others. Here we might begin by imagining their home life: What languages did these children regularly hear? They would have heard regularly Siamese and Chinese, and perhaps others. What does this mean? How did their grandparents dress? What games might they have played? What vocational alternatives did their relatives hold out to them? What kinds of stories did they hear and what kinds of literature did they emulate? How were their homes decorated? Some among them would regularly have seen Persians, Arabs, Indians of various sorts, Javanese, Malays, Bugis, and so forth. They might have had a very different idea of "foreign" than youngsters of a generation or two earlier.

It is usual to imagine that changes we imagine as "modern" began only in the nineteenth century, either in the decade following the Napoleonic era, or around the middle of the century. True, we lack much historical evidence from the previous century, but by the 1730s a new wave of prosperity and social variety had begun to sweep over at least the urban parts of Siam's society. It was not necessary to have the West present before major changes might overtake Siam.

THE LINGA GARDEN

IN THE MIDST OF ONE OF THE BUSIEST SECTIONS
of present-day Bangkok, there is a modern parking garage by
the side of an ancient but busy canal. By the exit ramp of that
garage, all but hidden from view, is a strange sight. Perhaps it
is neglected because it is forgotten. It should not be forgotten,
because its existence testifies to a revolution in modern Siamese
thought. More likely, it is neglected because it is considered
slightly embarrassing. It is a linga garden, that is, a place where
there are hundreds of wooden and stone objects that are phallic
in shape.

Plate 10 — The "linga garden" in
Bangkok (photo Wyatt 2000)

51

Why are they there? In a law promulgated on 21 August 1782,[1] the new king, Rama I (born in 1736 to a Thai father and a mother who was "daughter of a Chinese richest family")[2] ordered that all the phallic representations of the god Shiva should be gathered together and burned (ignoring the fact that many were of stone). He so decreed in order that the people of Siam should follow what he considered the "true" Way of Buddhism. This was necessary in order that a revived Siam might avoid the calamities that had beset the kingdom of Ayutthaya a generation earlier, when Siam had been attacked and utterly sacked by armies from Burma in April 1767. He also hoped to avoid the ridicule of foreign visitors. It is not difficult to imagine how he might have arrived at the former conclusion, as most of those present in the new Siam had lived through the calamities of the 1760s and 1770s, when hundreds of thousands died of starvation and violence.[3] But what foreign visitors might have ridiculed Siamese religious practices? And why might the new king have feared their ridicule?

King Rama I and many of his contemporaries in effect were voicing their own discomfort, perhaps embarrassment. They had gone through great pain and distress when the Burma forces had attacked and sacked Ayutthaya, and those who remained to assume power were young. Many Thai who remained were divided into plundering bands who beset the

---

1. *Kotmai tra sam duang* (Bangkok: Khurusapha, 1962) *V*, 320–325; or *Rüang kotmai tra sam duang* (Bangkok: Fine Arts Dept., 1978), pp. 754–756.

2. Sir John Bowring, *The Kingdom and People of Siam* (reprint edition; Kuala Lumpur: Oxford University Press, 1969), I, p. 66.

3. See David K. Wyatt, "The 'Subtle Revolution' of King Rama I of Siam," *Studies in Thai History* (Chiang Mai: Silkworm Books, 1996), pp. 131–172; first published in 1982.

countryside.[4] Those who came to power were unusually young by the customary standards of Siam. One of the half-Chinese boys who grew up in privileged families in Ayutthaya in the 1730s was named Sin, remembered as King Taksin (b. 1734; r. 1767–1782). In the short run, he was an exceptionally able organizer and leader, sweeping his armies across much of central Indochina, but toward 1780 he became megalomaniacal, and pretended to such divinity that he alienated many of his contemporaries. The formal explanation of what then happened is that a spontaneous rebellion erupted early in 1782 which swept the young king from the throne and then executed him. Another version of events has it that an able young Chiang Mai woman married to the younger brother of the future King Rama I helped organize the rebellion.[5] Whatever the actual list of participants, the real point of the story is that basic religious issues motivated the change of reign. Both Taksin and the future Rama I and his brother were active proponents of reformist Buddhism that blamed the kingdom's 1767 fall upon religious issues and sought to establish new Buddhist values that would correct the mistaken views of the past and ensure that the kingdom would not fall again. Taksin's solution was to make of himself a "stream-winner" on his way to personal buddhahood. Rama I, his brother (and siblings), and many others of their contemporaries wanted instead a "return" to a more rigorous Buddhism. It was from such sentiments that the "linga garden" was born.

---

4. Conditions at the fall of Ayutthaya are detailed by Rama I's own sister, Krommaluang Narinthewi, *Chotmaihet khwamsongcham* (Bangkok: Privately Printed, 1973); and a contemporary monk, Somdet Phra Wannarat, *Sangkhitayawong* (tr. Phraya Pariyathammathada; Bangkok: Crem. Phra Upalikhunupamachan, 1978), pp. 418–424.

5. *Chiang Mai Chronicle*, 2nd ed., p. 156.

It is the rationality and "scientific" attitude that seems so characteristic of the generation that came to power by the 1780s. In the past I have noted how the author of the laws of the period demonstrated their reasons. We might also, however, draw our attention to the audience that presumably "read" or had read to them the laws that came to them in a flurry in the First Reign of the new dynasty. After all, if you think of it, laws issued in the name of an absolute monarch did not have to have reasons: they might just be issued with absolute authority. If new actions had to be justified, then something was going on in the minds of at least some significant portion of the public. Surely it says something significant that all the laws of Siam were revised and reissued in 1805.

This leads us again back to the mind-set of the generation of King Rama I—and note again that we need to think about a substantial element of the population, and not just the ruler or his close associates. Let us begin by visualizing them. They appear in crowds on the murals painted on the walls of the new temples that adorned Bangkok. The first thing we note about them is their variety. Their complexions are dark and light and everything in between. Their hair styles make it clear that some are of Chinese descent and others Indians or Thai, as does their dress. They lived in all kinds of dwellings, tiny or palatial, those of the rich and of the poor. Contrast these depictions with the people seen on the walls of other parts of the neighboring world, where everyone looks the same.

If we begin with such visual impressions, let us move on to consider the entertainments they might have experienced. Here the world is as varied as the urban world developing by the 1740s. Now move on to the literature they listened to and chanted and wrote. Their poetry was becoming, according to

Nidhi Eoseewong, linguistically much more like their spoken language than the literature of a few generations earlier. And the literary works now found in Bangkok (founded in 1782) were much more international than they used to be: there were now translations from Chinese, Mon, Burmese, Persian, Malay, and Javanese, among others. We have to assume that those who sponsored and paid for these works did so because they wanted what had been particularistic tastes to become universalistic tastes.

Most of the literature associated with the late Ayutthaya period of Siam had been destroyed and lost in the devastation of the 1760s, and it had to be re-created from scratch from the 1780s. That which had been memorized might simply be copied again; but to meet new needs and match new thoughts there was a massive outpouring of words—massive in spite of the fact that printing was not yet employed. A good example of such literary renewal was a new "Exegesis of the Three Worlds" produced on royal order by Phraya Thammapricha (Kæo) in 1802. Though based on a work five hundred years old, this amounted to a drastic recasting of traditional Buddhist cosmological thought. Whereas the older tradition had begun with the celestial world and worked its way down to the world of humans and the underworld, the new work reversed the old order to begin with humans and work upwards from there.[6]

The more pious among contemporaries may have believed that it was owing to renewed orthodoxy, but many more surely believed that Siam's success was due to leadership, organization,

---

6. *Traiphum lok winitchai* (Bangkok, 1913). This work is discussed in Wyatt, *Studies in Thai History*, pp. 150–152. A full version of the same text is given in *Traiphum lok winitchai katha* (3 vols.; Bangkok: Fine Arts Dept., 1977).

and military might. For most of the first twenty years of Bangkok's history, Bangkok was at war with the lands west of the mountains. These were concluded only when forces from the northern principality of Nan succeeded, where Chiang Mai had failed, in expelling Burma forces from the Kok River basin in the far north (around Chiang Sæn). (Nan thereby gained a degree of prestige, power, and independence that Chiang Mai never enjoyed.) During the same period, Bangkok forces came to dominate the country we now think of as Laos, as well as what are now the northeastern provinces (Isan), and even Cambodia.

One of the keys to Bangkok's success is strikingly represented in the literary *chef d'oeuvre* of the reign of Rama I's son, Rama II (b. 1782; r. 1809–1824). This was the Thai-language version of the Ramayana epic poem of India—modified from his royal father's version—most of the subcontinent editions of which have the hero Rama praying to the gods for assistance and, with their aid, triumphing over worldly foes. The version of the Second Reign, however, has Rama tricking the gods into aiding him. Just as in the Three Worlds cosmology, human beings were at the center of the world and in control of their own fate.

SEXUAL VARIANTS

ONE SHIBBOLETH OF "POLITICALLY CORRECT" discourse in contemporary Thailand is to argue that those who see homosexuality in premodern Thailand are arguing their own prejudices, and their lack of knowledge of Thai-language sources. Homosexuality, they argue, is a modern, recent importation from the West, and was never seen in premodern Thailand and Siam.

Among other things, this argument centers on a brief passage in a source on the history of Chiang Mai, which probably dates from 1827 or 1828. This chronicle (by an unnamed author) includes the following passage.[1]

> The king was still in the South when an inauspicious thing[2] occurred in his country. Villagers of the Ban Hon–Mæ Sa–Mæ Lim region, two women jealously were contesting the same woman and spread the lie that the Burmese were coming and would catch them. On the eleventh waxing of the ninth month, a Saturday (?22 July 1816), in the midnight watch, a commotion arose throughout the domain.

1. *Chiang Mai Chronicle,* 2nd ed., p. 201.
2. Called *hani;* something out of the ordinary that presages the decline of the domain, according to the teachings of King Mangrai. See Sommai Premcit, *Khamsòn Phraya Mangrai* (Chiang Mai, 1976), pp. 25–26.

The significance of this passage, of course, would seem to be that it indicates that lesbianism was present in Siam well *before* there was substantial contact with the West.

This has proven to be a highly contentious issue. The real issue, however, seems to get lost. The real issue is about what the language of the text actually says. The phrase "two women jealously were contesting the same woman" has been taken to have nothing to do with sex.

The problem is, most of the people arguing about the translation and interpretation of this passage are unable to read the original, which is written in the local dialect (*kam müang*) in Northern Thai script, which is not readable by Central Thai speakers who have not studied Northern Thai writing. I tried the passage on two (women) scholars for whom Northern Thai is their mother tongue: not only were they raised speaking it in a village, but both of them now teach the language. Both now insist on the sexual interpretation of the passage as given above. Both also now generously insist that there is ample literary evidence of (usually but not exclusively) male homosexuality in datable sources from the early nineteenth century and before; and they add that we can also find artistic evidence in temple murals and even in paper manuscripts (*kradat sa*), which might usefully reinforce the point here, were it not against the law to engage in such pornography!

But almost lost in the heat of the argument is the very basic question of *why* the passage is even included in the source. The key of the subject sentence—the first sentence in the quotation—has to do with an "inauspicious thing" occurring. There seem to be three possible interpretations. Was the relationship between the women the "inauspicious thing"? Or was the false rumor the "inauspicious thing"? Or was it the combination of the relationship and the rumor that was "inauspicious"?

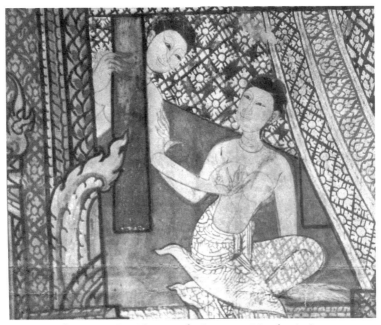

Plate 11 — Punishment of miscreants. Mural painting,
Wat Khongkharam, Ratchaburi.

We have to consider the possibilities in the context of the other things the author notes as being "inauspicious" in the course of chapter 8 of the chronicle. There are two other major such episodes. The first, ushering in an age of misfortune, occurs when there is conflict in 1823 between King Maha Suphathara and his brother, an episode which is concluded (at least temporarily) by a magical ceremony.[3] The second occurs a few years later when animals and disease signal the onset of an evil age in 1825–26.[4] Neither of these seems comparable to the false rumor and questionable relations in 1816. If not, then what is the author of the *Chiang Mai Chronicle* trying to communicate to his readers?

3. *Chiang Mai Chronicle*, 2nd ed., p. 208.
4. *Chiang Mai Chronicle*, 2nd ed., p. 211.

Plate 12 — Variant behavior. Mural, Wat Phumin, Nan.

I have long puzzled over this passage. I am persuaded that our translation (about homosexuality) is correct. I am certain that the author was involved in political disputes with the new ruler of Chiang Mai in 1817, and that he was using the writing of history to put forward his political argument subtly. I would like to be able to use his mention of the two women as an example of premodern laxity on the issue of homosexuality, which then we might use to argue that later similar circumstances were backed by similar laxity. However, there are similar cases that arise in 1848, the 1890s, and 1915, all of which suggest that Thai were not prepared always to regard such circumstances as irrelevant. What made all three of those episodes important had nothing to do with the sexual activities of those concerned. What was important was when the personal proclivities had political consequences.

The fact that the author of the chronicle did *not* make the 1816 circumstance a cause to introduce yet another Kali Age might at least encourage us to think that he thought the occurrence was worth noticing, but not worth drawing moral conclusions from it.

Plate 13 — Bangkok in 1822. From John Crawfurd, *Journal of an Embassy to the Courts of Siam and Cochin China* (London, 1828; repr. Kuala Lumpur: Oxford University Press, 1967), p. 78.

ECONOMIC CHANGES

AFTER A LONG PERIOD IN THE MIDDLE REGION
of the Malay Peninsula—especially in Kedah and in Nakhon
Si Thammarat—a British envoy arrived at Bangkok in
December 1825. This was Captain Henry Burney, and he
came with a long list of issues he wanted to settle with the rulers
of Siam. These fell generally into three broad categories: Anglo-
Siamese trade, particularly between newly-founded (1819)
Singapore and Bangkok; the Malay states, particularly as they
affected the security of British Penang; and the Anglo-Burmese
War (1824–26) and Siam's involvement in it.

In the British view, Singapore's trade and revenues were still
dangerously weak, and might benefit from liberalization of
Siamese trade. The security of Penang was still threatened by
continuing conflict with the Sultan of Kedah, a vassal of the
Siamese kings. The British wanted to remove him and pacify
the middle region of the Peninsula. Finally, in connection with
the Anglo-Burmese War, the British wanted to restore
population that had fled from peninsular Burma to Siam, to
obtain Siamese meat exports to feed their Indian troops in
Burma, and to obtain an alliance with Siam against Burma,
particularly when the war was not going well for the British.

Early negotiations between Burney and the Siamese were
contentious, as each side maneuvered for advantage against the

other. The Siamese, for example, agreed to cooperate against the Burmese if given a major base from which to operate in Peninsular Burma, including Tavoy and Martaban, while the British were trying to establish their own colonial possession from a base in exactly the same area. Burney noted that the Siamese were alarmed at the prospect of the British maltreating Burmese places of (Buddhist) worship.

In their first months of deliberations, little was gained by either side, mainly because of uncertainty as to how the war in Burma might turn out. Clearly the Siamese were divided over how to deal with the British. The Siamese position was strengthened by Burney's inclination to cede territory to them. Hesitating to press the Siamese on more delicate issues like trade, and relations with Burma, Burney concentrated mainly on "Burmese" (actually Mon) prisoners from Lower Burma who had fled to Siam in recent years.

The Siamese were themselves divided. King Rama III (b. 1787; r. 1824–1851) had many ambitious half-brothers around him, including even the sole surviving brother of King Rama I, Prince Itsaranurak, who himself had opposed Rama III's enthronement less than two years earlier. The government was dominated by a faction led by members of the Bunnag family, including the Kalahom (Ministry of the Southern Provinces and the Military), Phrakhlang (Ministry of Finance and Foreign Affairs) and the Phonlathep (Ministry of Lands). They were opposed by the Mahatthai (Ministry of the Northern Provinces), some princes, and many minor officials. Many of these were threatened by the issues Burney raised, either because they depended on revenues raised through trade (or by their control of commodities marketed by trade), or they depended on labor and manpower represented by Mon immigrants whom Burney wanted to send back to Burma.

News of the Treaty of Yandabo (24 February 1826) ending the First Anglo-Burmese War arrived in Bangkok only on 3 May, and the Siamese then moved immediately to bring to a head matters which Burney had been urging upon them for five months. All came to a head in a long meeting on the night of 14–15 May. Present on the Thai side were Prince Surin (1790–1830), and four ministers—the Chakri, Kalahom, Palace, and Phrakhlang ministers.

What accounts for the sudden Siamese about-face—their sudden reasonableness after months of stubbornness, in the British view? Clearly the exertion of British military power had made a difference, and the compelling factor was news that the British had forced the capitulation of the Burmese.

What we lack, however, is any indication of what the various Siamese might have been saying to each other. If we look at what they agreed to, and what they very quickly did, we are encouraged to imagine that a leading role was taken by the Phrakhlang (Dit Bunnag), who then was the leading member of the Bunnag family. Chairing the meeting was a half-brother of the Phrakhlang, whose wife also was a Bunnag woman; and the king then on the throne had a Bunnag mother. We can then begin by noting a strong familial connection.

Quite apart from all those assembled being among the most powerful men in the kingdom, at least two and probably three of them had immediate financial interests in the South and in the foreign maritime trade out of Bangkok. At the least, then, they were in a position to promise their fellow officials in other ministries that whatever cuts they might immediately have to make in the revenues from foreign trade, they could make up those losses. What they were prepared to undertake was that the losses might be offset by greater use being made of official monopolies. Over the decades to come, such monopolies would increasingly be expanded.

But the one thing the Siamese insisted upon was that they would not agree to the restoration of the Sultan of Kedah, who had been deposed and removed after colluding with the Burmese in previous years. This maintained the power and prerogatives of the Kalahom and the Phrakhlang, as well as Prince Surin.

Through this entire episode, and until the conclusion of a treaty with the British in July 1826, the Siamese were confirmed in the self-esteem which had been expressed earlier in the *Ramakian*. That is, they were warned that the world was a dangerous place, but that they could manage their own fate by the exercise of their native intelligence.

There were others, not so highly-placed, who might gain similar self-esteem in economic affairs. One particular town in what is now Northeast Thailand in the 1830s was given the option, because of its considerable distance from Bangkok, to pay its annual taxes either in cash or in kind, at its own option. The people there, even at that distance, quickly learned to watch the dockside price of that commodity in Bangkok. When the price was high, they sent their commodity to Bangkok and paid their taxes in cash from its sale. When the price was low, they paid their taxes in kind.[1]

The important point here is that economic sophistication was not limited to the high-ranking movers and shakers in the capital. What might seem like an inflexible, rigid economic system was capable of being very flexible.

1. Many fascinating details are given in Koizumi Junko, "The Commutation of *Suai* from Northeast Siam in the Middle of the Nineteenth Century," *Journal of Southeast Asian Studies* 23:2 (Sept. 1992), pp. 276–307.

POLICY ARGUMENTS IN CHIANG MAI

THE FIRST ANGLO-BURMESE WAR (1824–1826) DID not affect only the Burmese and the British, or even Siam. The international relations of all that part of the world were shaken profoundly. Siam had to re-think its relations with the British, and they had quickly, as we have seen, to come to terms with the British, who were their new neighbors to the West, across the mountains from Ratchaburi, Kanchanaburi, Phetchaburi, Chumphon, and Ranong. Obtaining inaccurate information, the Vientiane Lao launched a sudden military expedition against Bangkok in the so-called Lao-Thai War of 1826–27 which forever changed Lao history.

And far away to the north, leading figures in the kingdom of Lan Na, centered in Chiang Mai, were caught up in a fierce debate that must have nearly torn them apart. After the death of King Kawila (1782–1816), who had won independence after many generations of rule from Burma, the ruling family of Lan Na was torn asunder in what was nearly a civil war that ended with King Phutthawong (1825–1846) on the throne in Chiang Mai, but his defeated uncles and rivals still ruling in Lamphun and Lampang. Lan Na soon was affected by the Anglo-Burmese War right after it erupted in 1824. Chiang Mai often had been ruled by Burmese princes, and served as Burmese headquarters for their rule in Lan Na. Although the Lan Na people might have been tempted to get involved in that war, invariably on the side of Siam against Burma, they seem to have been more tempted to simply sit it out, particularly as a British victory became clearer by early 1826. That Chiang Mai faction might have been tempted to believe that a British victory would set Chiang Mai free. The Lan Na people repeatedly had suffered from the depredations of Burma armies, and now they need not worry about a security threat from the west. Similarly, they might no longer need to depend upon Bangkok, or upon Nan, for assistance against Burma. They were weak in Lan Na, and had had, for example, to depend upon armies from Nan to defeat the Burmese in Chiang Sæn in 1804.

Very few internal sources ever allude to the arguments that must have been raging through the winter months of 1826–27, and Bangkok sources are silent on the matter. All we know from Bangkok is that the Bangkok rulers were furious with Chiang Mai, irritated that Lan Na was not quickly sending an army to assist in the counterattack on Vientiane. Chiang Mai simply delayed as Bangkok's patience came near to breaking.

None of the sources tells us what the people in Chiang Mai were saying to each other. We are given only two hints as to what might have been going on there.

The first has to do with relations between the Lamphun people and the Chiang Mai people, representing Kawila's line and his brother's line, the latter of which had succeeded to the rulership in 1825. The Lamphun people were repeatedly reluctant to allow a visiting party from British Burma (led by David Richardson) to proceed on to Chiang Mai, despite repeated requests. Over the course of several visits by Richardson, it transpired that there were very bad relations between the two parties. The issue was how to treat Lan Na's new neighbor to the southwest—Britain in Martaban and south from there—and, more generally, how Lan Na might deal with foreign relations to its west. Here the Anglo-Burmese War had sharply refashioned the world for Lan Na in 1826.

Although it would be simplest to conclude that the bad blood between the two parties was a matter of dynastic rivalries, there is another interpretation that seems to make more sense.

This has to do with a curious historical writing produced by an unnamed person in 1827, just between the end of the Anglo-Burmese War and the first of Richardson's visits in 1829. The best guess is that the author of this work, the *Tamnan phün müang Chiang Mai* or *Chiang Mai Chronicle*, was a male, a person close to Chao Kawila, the first ruler of the new Chiang Mai. To him, all the history of Chiang Mai after the death of Kawila in 1816 was one calamity after another. He twice takes the opportunity to quote Kawila and Kawila's father *verbatim* on matters of state policy. The first quotation is to urge harmony and concord among the royal family.[1] The second quotation is another royal admonition to maintain royal unity and, especially, to maintain the strong alliance with the kings of Siam.[2]

It seems strange for the author to have broken his narrative twice to insert *verbatim* quotations; and we are left to wonder where these quotations might have come from. I am tempted to think immediately of historical arguments that began to break out in the 1960s, in which, to support their argument, historians would insert gratuitous quotations from the unchallengeable Prince Damrong Rajanubhab, even when they had to stretch historical memory to do so. It was as though they

---

1. *Chiang Mai Chronicle*, 2nd ed., pp. 164–165.
2. *Chiang Mai Chronicle*, 2nd ed., pp. 188–189.

might try to win their argument by retrospectively enlisting very high-ranking persons to do so.[3]

Here is a case where the intrusion of European power dramatically changed the existing balance of local power. In this case, the immediate outcome of the confrontation was determined by Bangkok, who settled the conflict with the Vientiane Lao by using little more than their own power in 1827, and then overcame local ineptitude in Chiang Mai by systematically usurping local power in the 1870s to 1890s.

3. This point is argued at greater length in David K. Wyatt, "Confronting the World and Each Other: Chiang Mai in the 1820s," *Moussons* [Marseilles], no. 99 (dècembre, 1999), 75–88.

THE BIBLIOPHILIC MONK

WHEN THINKING OF THE PEOPLES OF PREMODERN
Southeast Asia, we think of the word "peasant," and it is
difficult to move beyond that word to anything implying
intelligence. We do not usually associate the peoples of earlier
Southeast Asia with books, or reading, or writing. We might
pause when told that the male literacy rates of some parts of
Thailand in the 1890s were considerably in excess of the
literacy rates in Europe or America at the same time. In trying
to explain these and similar figures from neighboring parts of
Southeast Asia, we might begin by pointing to a cultural
pattern, by which most young freemen as boys entered the
Buddhist monkhood for a few years as a novice, to learn the
basic principles of their religion. In the process, they learned to
read and write.

We might expect that they learned to read and write from
perusing the Buddhist equivalent of the Old and New
Testament and other religious books. We might pause to
consider the enormous number of Buddhist temples that
included a library building. Even though modern (or any other
kind of) printing was not present in the Buddhist countries of
mainland Southeast Asia until the middle of the nineteenth
century or later, there were innumerable copies of texts incised
into palm leaves. The manuscripts were tied in bundles and

Plate 14 — Library at Wat Phra Sing, Chiang Mai (photo Wyatt 1988)

wrapped in cotton cloths and stored in temple libraries. Many such libraries lent out these manuscripts, while others had rigid rules prohibiting loans of books. The abbots of some temples were concerned about the damage that white ants might do to manuscripts and had a moat around the library to protect its contents.

The assembling of reading materials was not a modern innovation, for some manuscripts date from as long ago as five hundred years. Certainly up to about 90 percent of the manuscripts are religious, but that still leaves 10 percent that covered just about all other subjects, from poetry and other literature to law and medicine and history and veterinary science.

Before modern schools were introduced into remote rural provinces, all the local boys might learn to read and write in the village temple. Once schools were founded with Bangkok's support, they were not allowed to teach in the local dialects, and had instead to teach standard Bangkok Thai. Thus the last boys to be taught under the old system were those born by about 1920.

The boys who attended local temples there would have found numerous books, many probably copied for the purpose from copies in nearby temples. That is how, one imagines, that many copies of law books might be assembled for a community interested in that subject, or how a neighboring community might assemble its collection of manuscripts on another subject. But on the whole it is rare that we are told anything about how local library collections might have been assembled.

One major exception derives from the work of a Buddhist monk of the 1830s whom it is difficult not to think of as the "crazy bibliophile."[1]

1. Most of what I know about this monk's life and work was gained orally from M.R. Rujaya Abhakorn, my former student who at times has

Plate 15 — Library of Wat Sung Men, Phræ province, showing moat to protect manuscripts against white ants (photo Wyatt 1988)

---

been a professor of history and head of the library of Chiang Mai University. He was fascinated by the work of Khruba Kanchana, and took me to visit many places important in that monk's life and work. I have written briefly about Kanchana in "History and Directionality in the Early Nineteenth-Century Tai World," *The Last Stand of Asian Autonomies: Responses to Modernity in the Diverse States of Southeast Asia and Korea, 1750–1900,* ed. Anthony Reid (Basingstoke: Macmillan, 1997), 425–443, esp. 434–435.

This was the revered monk called Kanchana who usually was given the honorific prefix *khruba*. The story of Khruba Kanchana picks up at some time around 1830, when he was serving as the abbot of Wat Phra Sing, close to the center of old Chiang Mai. There he is said to have persuaded others, including the king of Lan Na, to construct a library at that temple, to hold the temple's manuscripts and to which many texts were then added. Under circumstances still not detailed, he had a falling out with his contemporaries, including the ruler of Lan Na and his fellow monks at Wat Phra Sing, and he left town.

Khruba Kanchana next turned up at the small village of Sung Men, just south of and close to the city of Phræ, where a minor king still was ruling. Becoming abbot of Wat Sung Men, he worked to get a number of important people, including the kings of Nan and Phræ, to sponsor the copying of manuscripts for a new library there which was inaugurated in 1837.[2] Copying there continued until as late as 1839. At Wat Sung Men, successive abbots are said to have had a strict rule prohibiting the lending out of manuscripts. Other libraries are often found denuded, which suggests that it was common for temple libraries to lend materials out, meaning that temple libraries must have functioned as public lending libraries.

At any rate, Khruba Kanchana again had a falling out with his friends and patrons in Phræ. This time he moved further south, becoming abbot of a temple in the vicinity of a town named Tak (the old town, not the new town of the same name). Again he built up a large library which, we are told, has never been unpacked, the palm-leaf manuscripts still sitting in

---

2. See Phouvong Phimmasone, "Cours de littérature lao," *Bulletin des Amis du Royaume Lao,* nos. 4–5 (Jan.–June 1971), pp. 16–17.

large chests raised high above the floor (which used to be regularly flooded by the Ping River).

It used to be fashionable to interpret actions like those of Khruba Kanchana as something like "whistling in the dark"— that is, acts that were committed knowingly in the face of impending doom, or at least change. It is true that, by the 1840s, there were a number of actions like the building of a stone Chinese junk at Wat Yannawa in Bangkok, or the engraved "university" at Wat Phra Chetuphon (Wat Pho), or even the last words of King Rama III, that might be interpreted that way. However, such interpretations are, in a way, melodramatic. The point to be underlined here is that it was normal for people to be bibliophilically crazy, or bookish. Thai poets and thinkers did not need the "inspiration" of the West to be intellectual.

THE WAT PHUMIN ARTIST

ONE OF THE BEST-KNOWN BUDDHIST TEMPLES in modern Thailand is probably also the least visited. This is the unusual quadrilateral Wat Phumin in the middle of the city of Nan, in extreme northern Thailand. It can be entered from each of the four cardinal directions, from each of which one enters to face the four central Buddha images. Once one has entered, one finds that the walls in the four directions are covered with mural paintings from foot-level to high above one's head, and the subject of the painting is unlike any other in the kingdom, based on the *Khatthanama-jataka*, which is not one of the 550 canonical Jataka, but one of a smaller set of extracanonical tales better known in the North. The real story of these wall-paintings, however, does not appear on the walls. It has to do with a message only being hinted at by what is on the walls. The story dates back to 1893.

By that time, King Chulalongkorn (Rama V, 1868–1910) had been on the throne of the kingdom of Siam for nearly a quarter of a century. His reign had not been quiet. He had succeeded his father when still a boy, and early on, he had struggled to wrest power from his relatives and from the old regent, who dominated the government until the mid-1880s. He had hardly established the progressive reign that he wanted when he was thrown into a short but nasty war with the

French, who overran Siamese army positions in Laos and then sent a naval force up the Chaophraya River to Bangkok. To forestall the French, King Chulalongkorn had to pay the French a huge indemnity, agree to punishment of the Siamese military for "murder" of a Frenchman in Laos, and agree to sign away all Siamese rights over the territory we now call Laos.

Forgotten in all the rhetoric we often see about the crisis of 1893 is the fact that Laos was not completely the property of Siam to be signed away. Extreme northern Laos, pretty much from Luang Prabang to Burma and China, did not technically belong to the king of Siam, but instead was part of the kingdom of Nan, and had been ruled effectively by the king of Nan since the beginning of the century.[1] On the death of Chao Ananta (1853–1891), his son, Chao Suliyaphong (1891–1918), succeeded him as king of Nan. The late king was cremated in May of 1893, and the new king almost immediately was faced with the loss of half his territory to the French.

Chao Suliyaphong does not seem to have been consulted by Bangkok when half his territory was taken from him and given to the French. He understood much better than the rulers of Chiang Mai how important it was to remain a subsidiary of Siam, even despite the ignominy of 1893. But what was the ruler of Nan to do? He could not criticize Bangkok in public, and he could not even voice his pain in public. He could only do what generations of Thai had done.

Chao Suliyaphong quickly did two things that only subtly indicated his displeasure. First, he commissioned the writing of a new history of Nan, by Sænluang Ratchasomphan.[2] At first

---

1. See David K. Wyatt, *Temple Murals as an Historical Source: The Case of Wat Phumin, Nan* (Bangkok: Chulalongkorn University Press, 1993).

2. David K. Wyatt, tr., *The Nan Chronicle* (Ithaca, 1994).

glance, this looks much like earlier histories of Nan, and indeed it copies large portions from them. Looking particularly at the nineteenth-century portion, however, the whole seems to assume a character of its own. One quickly realizes that Nan is being portrayed as an "orphan" state, repeatedly bereft of its "father." First Sukhothai, then Chiang Mai or Lan Na, then the Burmese, and finally even Bangkok are portrayed as having assumed the role of "father" to Nan, but by the end of the book, all these "fathers" had abandoned their child. Even though the "crisis" of 1893 is not mentioned, even though the chronological span of the chronicle extends beyond 1893, it is hard to miss the fact that the author of the chronicle has deliberately adopted the "orphan" metaphor. Under the circumstances, it is difficult to avoid concluding that the author of the chronicle was deliberately steered in that direction.

It is all the more difficult to avoid that conclusion when we include in our purview the murals that decorate the walls of Wat Phumin. It has been argued that Wat Phumin's murals were painted at the same time as the building was constructed, in the 1860s. In addition to there being good reasons to associate the murals with the chronicle and the context of the 1890s, and there so far being no external evidence to testify that the murals were painted before at least the 1880s, it simply makes better sense to associate the murals with the 1890s than with the 1860s. We do know that, when the British consul visited from Chiang Mai in the 1880s, the murals still were not mentioned, though the visitor went there.

We know that the mural paintings at Wat Phumin were painted by the same artist as the person who painted the murals at Wat Nong Bua, which is about 40 kilometers (25 miles) north of Nan city; and we know that they were not painted by the same person who painted the murals at Wiang Ta in Phræ

Plate 16 — Artist and his lady friend.
Painting copied from Wat Phumin mural. Private collection.

province. Moreover, the Nong Bua murals apparently were painted by direct commission from the authorities there, which leads us to suppose that the Wat Phumin murals were painted later, probably on the recommendation of someone who had seen Wat Nong Bua. (The Nan royal family is said to have had a summer palace in nearby Tha Wang Pha.)

I am led to believe that the Wat Phumin artist was of Tai Lü descent, probably associated with Lü immigrants who came south from Sipsong Panna earlier in the century, whose stone irrigation works are still to be found in the village associated with Wat Nong Bua. We do not know the name of the painter who produced the murals, but we do have what purports to be a portrait of him, a portrait of a man courting a woman, which some have said is the artist's "escort" of the evening![3]

What makes these paintings at Wat Phumin most relevant is the fact that, illustrating the Jataka story of Khatthanama, they happen to concentrate on one of the rare Jataka stories that centers on the issue of orphanhood. This hardly seems a coincidence, particularly in the context of the contents of the *Nan Chronicle*, which I believe to have been composed at about the same time.

In the cases both of the *Nan Chronicle* of Sænluang Ratchasomphan and the Wat Phumin murals executed by the anonymous Lü artist, we are dealing with commissioned art works that deal with orphanhood. This is all the more interesting in the light of later use of Jataka stories.

---

3. Both sets of murals are the subject of *Wat Phumin and Wat Nong Bua* (Bangkok: Muang Boran, 1986). This volume includes many color plates. A good contemporary account of Nan is in Reginald Le May, *An Asian Arcady: The Land and Peoples of Northern Siam* (1926; reprint Bangkok: White Lotus, 1996), pp. 163–177.

MODERN HISTORIANS

BY THE TURN INTO THE TWENTIETH CENTURY, a handful of individuals were writing modern history— modern, that is, in terms of how it was structured rather than what it covered. One of them was a member of a long-term noble family, while the other was probably a Lao. Both got started writing right at the turn of the century. Both professed a real interest in evidence, though they differed in how they treated it.

Phraya Prachakitkòrachak (Chæm Bunnag, 1864–1907) was indeed a member of the illustrious Bunnag family, and a grandson of Chaophraya Prayurawong (Dit Bunnag), and the son of a half-brother of the eminent Chaophraya Sisuriyawong (Chuang), namely Phra Phrommathiban (Chon).[1] He began his education near the Grand Palace in Bangkok, and soon entered the staff of the Supreme Court (*San Dika*). Having gained the attention of the king's brother, Prince Phichit, he served a brief period in Chiang Mai in 1883–84. By 1886 he was back in Chiang Mai on legal work, and he seems to have begun by this time his habit of studying local Tai languages

---

1. I have depended heavily here upon an unpublished paper by Akiko Iijima, "The *Phongsawdan Yonok* as Part of Modern Siamese Historiography" (Tokyo, 1993).

and writing systems. He had a genuine interest in the people the Siamese termed "Lao" which included both the Mekong peoples and the Tai Yuan of the Chiang Mai and adjacent regions. He was hotly engaged in military conflict with the French in 1893, which gained him promotion to the exalted rank of *phraya* at the tender age of thirty years in 1894. He spent the remainder of his short life in legal work mostly in Bangkok until his death there at the age of merely forty-three in 1907.

Right now, we do not have definite information on all Phraya Prachakit's activities in the North, but it seems likely that among his early duties was looking after the activities of the British spy, George Younghusband. He may, indeed, have had a role in several plots to interfere with the mission of Younghusband in 1886–1887.[2] We can judge from his early activities that Phraya Prachakit had exceptional language skills and was a quick learner of the cultures and personalities he encountered in the North.

At best, Phraya Prachakit may have had only twenty years of adult productivity. However, he wrote quite a lot, especially on the history of the North. He is best remembered for his *Phongsawadan Yonok*, which began a long publishing history serialized in the magazine *Wachirayan* in 1898–99. It was based on local manuscripts, most of them either in Tai Yuan language and script, or in Pali. It gained admission to the prestigious

2. See G. J. Younghusband, *Eighteen Hundred Miles on a Burmese Tat Through Burmah, Siam and the Eastern Shan States* (London: W. H. Allen, 1888; reprinted New Delhi: Asian Educational Services, 1995); and Younghusband's own *The Trans-Salwin State of Keng Tung* (Calcutta, 1887; repr. ed. D. K. Wyatt and Tej Bunnag; Chiang Mai: Silkworm Books, forthcoming), which includes much additional information in the editor's preface.

Plate 17 — K.S.R. Kulap and his son Chai, in their book
Mahamukkhamattayanukunlawong [Great Ministerial Families]
(Bangkok, 1905), p. 15.

Prachum Phongsawadan (Collected Chronicles) in volume 5, published in 1917, long after its author's death in 1907. Many of its points have since been contested, but it has been reprinted countless times, even up to recent years. It is worth noting that few subsequent historians have taken Northern Thai historical sources seriously.

Phraya Prachakit was not alone. There was a substantial number of his fellow historians by the turn of the century. There were many high-born nobles and princes among them, but few could have been as colorful as K.S.R. Kulap, or Kulap Kritsananon (1834–ca. 1913). Like many of his contemporary intellectuals, he was a member of the elite Library Society (which ultimately would be transformed into the National Library). He first gained substantial bibliographical experience, and contact with highly-placed Thai officials and princes, at the centennial exposition celebrating the dynasty's centenary in 1882.

Kulap was "crazy" about books, not so much like Khruba Kanchana, but in a way that gave him a sort of power socially that he could not otherwise have gained. Birth did not give him privileged access to power, nor did bureaucratic office. Descended from an old noble family perhaps from the Northeast, he had a decent if sporadic monastic education. He had a respectable career through middle age in the Harbor Police, and in various foreign firms, all of which strengthened his language skills. But he made his mark especially as a publisher in his old age, running a periodical called *Sayam Praphet.* In its pages, and in the separate books he published, he showed a special interest in the history of the great families who so dominated his age. From many he borrowed manuscripts now otherwise lost, from which for example we are given many details of the history of Chinese immigration in the eighteenth century.

As an historian, however, Kulap fell considerably short of perfection. He was careless with his sources, which he was prone to embellish. Such carelessness and dishonesty got him into trouble, ultimately in legal charges of which authorities found him guilty in 1901, but refrained from putting him in jail on account of his advanced age.[3]

Without really saying so, both Phraya Prachakit and K.S.R. Kulap were through their work saying that the study of history —or at least some awareness of the past—was especially important to a generation that was rushing headlong into the future. Whether writing as Kulap did about old elite groups and ethnic minorities like Chinese, or about regional minorities in the North and Northeast as Phraya Prachakit did, both were expressing their hopes for the social and political inclusion of people who might otherwise get shoved aside.

3. See Craig J. Reynolds, "The Case of K.S.R. Kulap: A Challenge to Royal Historical Writing in Late Nineteenth Century Thailand," *Journal of the Siam Society* 61:2 (July 1973), pp. 63–90.

EDUCATION AND CHULALONGKORN

KING CHULALONGKORN (RAMA V, B. 1853, R. 1868–1910) was on the throne for a very long time—forty-two years. Many of them were not happy years. The reign began with serious conflict between the young king and his regent, and then between the king and the senior officials who remained in place. There were major conflagrations in 1875 and again in 1879; and Chulalongkorn even considered abdication and exile abroad around 1880. But all died down just as quickly as it had begun when the senior officials began quickly to die off in the 1880s.

From about 1885, the king began to refashion his government radically. He moved to a cabinet form of government, with functional distribution among the ministries. The new system began from 1892, eventually with twelve ministries. But the new government soon was thrown into crisis with a brief war with France, as a result of which Siam had to pay an enormous indemnity, yield the distant east bank of the Mekong River to French Indochina, and agree to prosecute the Thai military who had bravely defended the country against France.

Within the last two decades of the reign, between 1890 and 1910, Siam was transformed into something resembling modern Thailand, with modern ministries of Defense, Foreign Affairs, Finance, Agriculture, Interior, Education, Public Works, and so forth. With greatly increased public revenues, they could tie the country together with new railways and the rudiments of new institutions. It was all the easier for Chulalongkorn to accomplish this after he undertook his first trip directly abroad, to Europe, in 1898. This trip must have had an impact on him, for the decisions he made upon his return betrayed a new independence, which surprisingly went against what his European advisors were telling him. One of the earliest such decisions was in the area of education.

Cecil Carter, among several Europeans working in the field of education, urged him to create a boarding school in Bangkok, modeled on schools in Europe intended for the élite. We might expect the king to go along with such suggestions, short as he was of high-level administrators for his depleted élite of bureaucratic administrators. Instead, Chulalongkorn chose to democratize his administration by widening the recruitment of new, young men for his bureaucratic élite.[1]

Many actions taken by King Chulalongkorn, all of which demonstrated his vision of a future for his kingdom, departed from the policies of previous kings and ministers. Many of these reflected his desire to emulate, or even to exceed, what he had seen in the West. Many of these involved education, for the king and his advisors knew well that it would take educational reform to make a nation out of what had long been a kingdom.

---

1. See D. K. Wyatt, *The Politics of Reform in Thailand* (New Haven: Yale University Press, 1969), p. 333; and the same author's "King Chulalongkorn the Great: Founder of Modern Thailand," *Asia* [Asia Society, New York], Supplement 2, (Spring 1976), pp. 5–16.

Take, for example, the new policies that required that the government would support only education in Central (Standard) Thai language and script. Behind this policy lay the

Plate 18 — School in Nongkhai province, ca. 1928? From Ebbe Kornerup, *Friendly Siam* (New York: Putnam, 1928?), p. 114.

idea that Siam would require communications in a single, standard language—and even that all schools would have to teach its modern subjects (history, arithmetic, civics, etc.) uniformly, the same in the North and Northeast as in the Central and Southern parts of the country.

This paralleled a similar effort, spearheaded by the king's younger half-brother, who was supreme patriarch of the Buddhist establishment, to make even the established religion uniform, and responsible to a single set of ecclesiastical authorities in Bangkok.[2]

It would take generations for these innovations to make their presence felt throughout the kingdom. There was another policy reform that worked more quickly. This had to do with the age-old practice of levying taxes in cash, in kind, and even in labor. It had long been customary for men between the ages of twenty-one and sixty to render three or four months' service each year, either to some patron, or to "the government." After years of talking about it, in 1905 the government suddenly announced the ending of compulsory labor service. It would take a decade or more before this policy was applied everywhere.

The compulsory labor service was replaced by the government hiring of laborers to undertake such public works projects as digging canals.

Meanwhile, the labor demands of the military, which were relatively minor, were met by limited conscription.

With streets and roads stretching throughout the city, and a modern government now in place, by the end of his reign in

2. See Kamala Tiyavanich, *Forest Recollections: Wandering Monks in Twentieth-century Thailand* (Honolulu: University of Hawaii Press, 1997; Chiang Mai: Silkworm Books, 1997).

1910 King Chulalongkorn could have taken some comfort in thinking that his kingdom was well on the way to modernity. When he decided that his job was not to emulate the colonial possessions like Burma, Malaya, the Straits Settlements, and India, but rather the home countries like Britain and France, little could he imagine what was just around the corner.

Plate 19 — Vajiravudh and some of his pages. From cover photography, S. L. W. Greene, *Absolute Dreams* (Bangkok: White Lotus, 1999).

THE ABSOLUTE MIKADO

VAJIRAVUDH WAS NOT HIS FATHER'S FIRST CHOICE to succeed to the throne, but Crown Prince Vajirunhis died prematurely at the age of seventeen in 1895, when his younger brother already had gone off to school in England. Chulalongkorn apparently felt he had no choice but to proceed to the next in line for the throne. Vajiravudh seems to have been more interested in literary and dramatic activities, and it was these that particularly occupied him upon his return from abroad in 1903.

Established in Saranrom Palace, across the road from Chulalongkorn's Grand Palace, Vajiravudh had his own large entourage, including a military contingent of adjutants and pages. There, he wrote and staged his own plays, "played" at government by setting up his own miniature city and country, and edited and published his own newspapers and magazines.

Vajiravudh's palace was not far from the Military Academy, and the young men from the two camps often got together. One day the cadets from the two groups got in a fight, and the young military men complained to the crown prince, expecting that the young pages would be punished, or at least disciplined. That did not happen, and from then on, there was bad blood between the two groups.[1]

1. My chief source is the memoir by Rian Sichan and Net Phunwiwat,

Relations between the two groups worsened after Vajiravudh succeeded his father in October 1910. Within the first few months, it became clear that Vajiravudh (Rama VI, r. 1910–1925) was proposing his pages and retainers for military promotion, in preference to the young military officers who normally might have expected promotion. The military were all the more antagonized when the king founded the so-called Wild Tiger Corps, a paramilitary organization that took the leading role in the young king's experiments with nationalism. What had begun as a "gripe group" became a group of conspirators planning a *coup d'état*, all the more seriously as the young men began to fear discovery. Their arguments ranged widely, but soon they came to focus particularly on the identity of the next king—for they could agree on no alternative to monarchy. They were singularly silly in settling on the king's younger brother, Prince Chakkrapong, who then was head of the army. When some of the more zealous among the conspirators told the prince of their plans, he chartered a railway train and sped away to the seaside resort, Hua Hin, and told Vajiravudh what had been discovered.

Justice and punishment were swift. The junior conspirators were sentenced to prison terms, but the senior conspirators were sentenced to death. They were reprieved at the last moment, but sentenced to life imprisonment.

It is said by some that a second military coup against Vajiravudh was attempted in 1917, but there is no definite evidence of this. And we know that resistance—especially senior and military resistance—was rampant from about 1915 onwards. In the face of continuing resistance, we might expect

---

Mò Leng ramlük: Phak patiwat khrang ræk khòng Thai R.S. 130 (Bangkok: Crem. Khun Thuaihanphithak, 1960).

Plate 20 — Cartoon of King Vajiravudh from *Dusit Samit*. From W. F. Vella, *Chaiyo!* (Honolulu: University of Hawaii Press, 1978), p. 65.

the young king—educated abroad—to have moved to lighten the reins of regal autocracy. He did not. Instead, he moved to strengthen the armed forces, led a public campaign to popularize nationalistic ideas, promoted and enriched some of his favorites, and even sent Siamese troops to fight on the Allied side in France in World War I.

Thai participation in World War I was especially interesting. While Vietnam sent hundreds of thousands of youth (including Ho Chi Minh) to serve as common laborers in France, the Siamese sent a squadron of aviators. So far as we know, no one said anything publicly about this symbolism, but none would be allowed to forget it when the war was over.

King Vajiravudh engaged in another bit of symbolism that was, again, so subtle that virtually no one noticed. Many years earlier, in 1890, King Chulalongkorn had sent some of his children to attend a special performance of musical theater in Singapore. There, they attended a performance of "The Mikado," by W. S. Gilbert and Sir Arthur Sullivan, which then was quite new (1885) and quite popular.

To reinforce their school lessons, the king had his children re-write the play in Thai. He was unhappy with the result, and himself wrote a version of the play in the form of Buddhist chanting. As a child, Vajiravudh must have been involved in this little exercise. It probably reinforced his dramatic interests, and perhaps even his inclination to write drama.

As king, Vajiravudh wrote two separate versions of "The Mikado."[2] The first is unremarkable. The second was an attempt to completely rewrite the play. Vajiravudh probably didn't know, as we do, that, though "The Mikado" is set in a mythi-

2. See D. K. Wyatt, "The Kings' Mikado," *Journal of the Siam Society* 81:1 (1993), pp. 131–137.

cal Japan, it really has nothing at all to do with Japan: it is about ordinary human beings, who find the Japanese to be rather mysterious beings. Rather than being Japanese, they poke fun at the Japanese, "who don't use pocket handkerchiefs."[3] Most interestingly, Vajiravudh rewrites "The Mikado" in such a way as to reveal his sentiments about monarchy.

At any rate, Vajiravudh now set "The Mikado" not in Japan but in some country that was more like Siam; and the monarch of "The Mikado" was absolute like the new author. Vajiravudh was anxious to modernize the play and his country; but he demonstrated no intention to dispense with the absolutism that held Siam together.

3. W. S. Gilbert, *The Savoy Operas* (London: Macmillan, 1968), "The Mikado," Act II, p. 361.

MODERNIZATION WITHOUT DEVELOPMENT

THOSE WHO HAVE STUDIED THE ECONOMIC
history of Thailand maintain that the country was economically static from the last years of the reign of King Chulalongkorn until the early 1950s. There is much to commend
this view, including the paucity and unreliability of statistics
before the 1960s, and the severe damage inflicted on the Thai
economy by the ravages of World War II. (The war, for example, brought the pillaging of the south Thailand railway
system, including the removal of most of its trackage, in order
to build the infamous "Death Railway" between Siam and
Burma.)

In looking at the decades from the beginning of the First to
the beginning of the Second World War: there is much we
might see that would reinforce the view of Siam's economic
stasis. We might begin with the kingdom's finances. The
nation had run up a considerable debt, in part to complete an
enormous shopping list of capital expenditures, like the
extension of the railway system to the North and South, and
covering enormous expenditure overruns during Vajiravudh's
reign. This hit most heavily in the years immediately following
the First World War, just at a time when the world economy
went into a short depression.

The Thai economy barely had recovered from this economic

shock when the reign of Vajiravudh unexpectedly ended on his death in late 1925, and his younger brother Prajadhipok began his reign with a commitment to drastic budget-cutting. This policy shift had barely taken hold under Prajadhipok (who admitted that he did not understand economics) when the country was hit with the great World Depression, which began in 1929 and struck Siam the following year.

One of the casualties of this belt-tightening was a dramatic decline in government spending. With this went, of course, a sharp fall in government income. The rural situation was not nearly as bad as it was in neighboring British Burma, where taxes were higher and agricultural indebtedness—which had to be paid off to (mostly) immigrant moneylenders—was more severe. Farmers still had to sell their rice to gain the income they needed to pay their taxes and buy their imported goods (like kerosene), but they were not dependent on such income to the same extent as in Burma.

Given this situation, and the hard years of the Japanese occupation still ahead, it would not be difficult to understand the no-growth years that Sompop and others have seen.[1] In fact, it would not have been surprising to find that Siam had regressed economically in the 1930s. However, let us look ahead at the weak figures that are still appearing in the 1950s. Why might a defense be mounted of Siam's economic performance?

The positive developments that occurred in Siam between the end of the First World War and the beginning of the Second were social, political, and cultural. Here we should begin by remembering that Chinese immigration to Siam

1. Sompop Manarangsan, *Economic Development of Thailand, 1850–1950* (Bangkok: Institute of Asian Studies, Chulalongkorn University, 1989).

Plate 21 — "Chinatown," on Yaowarat Road, ca. 1930. From Thepchu Thapthong, *Krungthep nai adit* (Bangkok: Aksonbandit, 1975), p. 208.

reached its peak around 1930. Since most such immigrants reached Bangkok, we might suppose that most immigrants simply added to the poorest section of the city's population. But note that most Chinese were young men without families, and might have been expected to be approaching their most productive years. Chinese amounted to around 12 percent of the population of Siam, but it is fair to assume that most of them were concentrated in Bangkok, where they were around 40 percent or more of the population. Presumably they were not bound to family lands or property, and might be assumed to have been available for entrepreneurial roles.

Bangkok presumably reached the pinnacle of its "Chineseness" around 1930. Chinese dress and behavior filled the streets; and even thirty years later there would be some portions of the city that were noticeably Chinese. Most businesses, retail and wholesale, were dominated by Chinese, as were some professions, from prostitution to watch repair. The city was residentially segregated, with Thai in some sections and Chinese in others, while residential settlement was also divided by socioeconomic class.

But the Chinese were hardly alone. Particularly when the world depression forced some Thais to leave the countryside in search of income, many (both men and women) came to Bangkok. Many took work as pedicab drivers, seamstresses, barbers, groundskeepers, prostitutes, drivers, and the like. This is not to argue that the world depression was "good" because it encouraged people to leave agriculture. It is simply to argue that, even though the depression brought with it pain, suffering, poverty, hunger, loneliness, and the like, it also gave some people a broadened range of experience, including wage labor and living in cities.

In 1932, an elite military "revolution" ended the absolute

monarchy and instituted what called itself a "popular" government but soon became a military dictatorship. The "Promoters," as they called themselves, based their rule on reducing royal and princely privileges, on reducing Chinese economic power, and on improving educational and health standards for the masses of the population.

Modern medicine, which started earlier with medical missionaries and health dispensaries, and with major Rockefeller Foundation support of the Siriraj Hospital, got an important boost from military support in the 1930s, although it still was concentrated almost exclusively in Bangkok.

A modicum of modern education was expressly promised to the general population in the early constitutions. Indeed, the constitution of 1932 promised that the national assembly would be fully elected after mass literacy had been achieved by 1942. From the beginning, suffrage was extended to both men and women who were literate.

Thus the Promoters began with a commitment to education—including the education of women—and to their credit they worked seriously to make substantial educational improvements. The results can be seen in a careful analysis of the 1960 census, which was the first fully accurate census. There, one is struck by a rapid increase in female literacy, from less than half of those who would have gone to school before 1926 to 70 percent of those who would have gone to school in the early 1930s and above 80 percent of those who would have gone to school by the mid-1930s.[2]

It is hard to argue against the economists who point at the numbers from 1910 and 1950 to prove that Siam hardly

2. *Thailand Population Census 1960, Whole Kingdom* (Bangkok: Central Statistical Office, 1962), p. 20.

"modernized" in the interval. At the same time, there are many ways in which we can see that the Thailand of 1950 is hardly the same country as the Siam of 1910. The real difference is "inside the heads" of millions of people, men and women. The difference is in the education, the literacy and the numeracy, as well as in the interpersonal relations. It is qualitatively similar to explaining why the Siam of Rama I (in 1782) was possible because of the changes that had been occurring since the reign of King Borommakot half a century earlier.

Plate 22 — Schoolgirls at the turn of the century. From Cecil Carter, *The Kingdom of Siam* (New York: Putnam, 1904), p. 208.

SOGGY HORSE

IN FEBRUARY 1988, A GROUP OF SMUGGLERS
moved a shipment of heroin (sometimes referred to as "horse"),
a white powder packed in polyethylene bags, southward along
the eastern frontier of Burma, and then entered Thailand from
the Tenasserim hills to a locality somewhere in the region of
Chumphon. There they unpacked the narcotics from the
horsebacks on which it had ridden, and then ladled it in thin
layers between sheets of raw rubber. They were operating on
the theory that dogs sniffing for heroin either in the shipping
warehouses at the Thai end, or at the American warehouses in
the Port of New York, to which the heroin was destined, would
not be able to sniff the heroin, masked as it was by the pungent
scent of rubber.

The sheets of raw rubber then were sent by truck, or perhaps
by train, to the warehouses of Khlong Toey, the Port of
Bangkok. There they were stacked to await shipment to New
York. Authorities later estimated that the value of the heroin
was something approaching 2 billion dollars on the street in
New York.

The theory was good. Perhaps it was based on past successes,
of the shipment of heroin, perhaps in smaller quantities. (It is
difficult to imagine that they would have risked such a huge

monetary investment without having first tested the procedures on a smaller quantity.)

But this time something happened that the smugglers had not counted upon. One story has it that the warehouse in which the shipment lay had a leaky roof, and let in quite a lot of water during the last weeks of the heavy monsoon rains. The water mixed with the heroin powder and ran out onto the floor, and there it soon was located by the drug-sniffing dogs who patrolled the warehouse. The police were called in, and then the newspapers; and soon the media were filled with stories about the enormous drug haul.[1] The press in subsequent months did not report the burning of the seized heroin, although that would have been done thirty years earlier under similar circumstances (but with much smaller quantities).

A similar story has it that the customs authorities soon noticed that some "rubber" bales were much heavier than others (because of the heroin tucked inside), and they opened a few heavier bales to discover the drugs hidden inside. That in turn led them to open all the bales of "rubber" and uncover all the drugs hidden inside.

It was the magnitude of the drug shipment that some found surprising. *Two billion* dollars is a very substantial sum of money, equal to something like 1.5 percent of the total Thai exports of goods in those days.[2] It destroyed the illusion that we might be thinking about a minor illegal activity, carried on by just a few people on the fringes of the society. No, people do not deal with billions, or even tens or hundreds of millions,

1. See "1,280 kilos of heroin seized at Klong Toey," *Bangkok Post,* February 13, 1988, p. 1.

2. All exports amounted to nearly 300 billion baht value in 1987. Thailand, National Statistical Office, *Statistical Yearbook Thailand 1994* (Bangkok, 1994), p. 247.

Plate 23 —
Rubber bales
containing heroin
split open at
Bangkok docks
(*Bangkok Post*)

of dollars, by employing just a handful of people. With such quantities of money, we must assume that large numbers of people were involved.

Moreover, such enterprises do not come and go overnight. They take many years to become established, both in developing (so to speak) the market and in serving the demand. In thinking about this matter, we might go back to the days of the opium monopoly in Thailand, which lasted to the 1950s.[3] In its day, the Opium Monopoly (or Opium Régie, as it was sometimes called) accounted for as much as 20 percent of the national budget of Thailand, though the numbers declined rapidly after World War II.[4]

3. The only discussion I can find in my home library is in Virginia Thompson, *Thailand: The New Siam* (New York: Paragon, 1967), pp. 726–743. Surely there are other discussions elsewhere, which might give estimates of opium's total contributions to the state revenues.

4. Detailed figures are given in the *Statistical Yearbook Thailand,* noting especially the volumes for 1937–38 and 1938–39 (no. 20), and 1939–40 to

Older folks will tell of having walked past opium "dens" or "parlors" in their youth on the streets of Bangkok. But I am more interested here in the heroin trade, involving an item more easily transported and traded, an item which is associated with the post–World War II period in world history. Much has been said about the opium trade of Laos, and about how opium became associated with the involvement in the Indochina War of the Hmong (Meo) people, who are its primary growers and inhabit that portion of the world in which opium is best grown.[5]

Nowadays, opium is most clearly associated with the area known as the "Golden Triangle," the mountainous and thinly-settled territory in the extreme north of Thailand, the northeast of Burma, and the northwest of Laos. Here is where the Thai come in—quite literally!

When the Japanese invaded Thailand on their way to Burma and Singapore on 8 December 1941, they soon were in a position where they were persuaded to offer Thailand various benefits to encourage their participation in the war as Japan's ally. The authorities in Thailand explained that, under wartime conditions, Thailand now was cut off from its supplies of opium from India, and the Japanese were led to see that the deficit might be made up by opium grown in northeastern Burma—the Shan States. This was not a trivial matter: before the war, the Government Opium Monopoly had contributed

---

1944 (no. 21). Subsequent issues omit mention of the opium monopoly. Comparative figures for government income (uncorrected for inflation) are given in a table for 1892 to 1950 in James C. Ingram, *Economic Change in Thailand, 1850–1970* (Stanford: Stanford Univ. Press, 1971), p. 185.

5. Alfred W. McCoy, *The Politics of Heroin in Southeast Asia* (New York: Harper & Row, 1972; rev. ed. Chicago: Lawrence Hill Books, 1991).

a substantial share of the total government revenues. By August 1943, the Japanese were prevailed upon to cede to Thailand the Shan States, as well as the northern portions of Malaya (now Perlis, Kedah, Kelantan, and Trengganu).

The now-strengthened Thai army was sent up to occupy the Shan States, now renamed Thai Doem, with a capital at Keng Tung. They quickly got to know that their near neighbor, just across the border in the Yunnan province of China, was the 93rd Division of Chiang Kai-shek's Kuomintang Army. Despite being formally enemies, the Thai were on good terms with their Chinese military opponents. Common gossip reports that whenever the Thai army learned that the Japanese were coming up to inspect the frontier, the Thai and Chinese would carry out a mock battle, often with blank ammunition. The Japanese were impressed. When the World War II (1945), and the civil war in China (1949), ended, the friendship between the Thai and Chinese military forces continued. Some of the 93rd Division forces were resettled in a village in Chiang Rai province, Mæ Salòng. It was from such positions in Thailand that air-drops to KMT forces in Burma continued for some years, and from which reconnaissance forays (on behalf of the United States) into the People's Republic of China were carried on.

It would strain credulity to imagine that certain Thai military (and police) did such things out of the goodness of their hearts or the strength of their anti-communist zeal. The Thai had their own shopping lists of things their forces needed or riches they coveted; and increasingly they had their own "business" to be carried on in organizing and transporting and marketing drugs from their former positions in the Shan States, and on behalf of their clients in Mæ Salòng.

Some of the Thai military who had been stationed in Keng Tung and the vicinity during the war, continued after the war, and were enriched by their "business."[6] My theory—and it is nothing but a "theory"—is that, from the mid- to late-1940s until at least the beginning of the twenty-first century, there has always been what I might call a "bag-man" in the Thai military establishment. By this, I mean that the enterprise generated a lot of money, but also spent a lot of money; and someone was needed to distribute the money among those who needed to be "cut in" on the enterprise.

There are unconfirmed rumors that shipments of drugs from North Thailand for embarkation abroad from Bangkok were escorted by military and paramilitary forces, or even that they were transported in military trucks! More to the point are unconfirmed stories of major movements of cash to those in high military and political positions. It is even said that elections have been affected by such cash, and that warfare has been conducted in the interest of such enterprises.

6. A thorough study of Thai military dispositions during the Thai Indochina War (1940–41) and the Greater East Asia War (1941–1945) is contained in a document from Thai military sources, translated and of unknown provenance in the Cornell University Library, *The Unit Organization [of the Royal Thai Army] during the Indo-China Conflict and the Great East Asian War*, prepared under the auspices of the Office, Chief of Military History by Operations Division, Royal Thai Army (Bangkok, ca. 1949?), 2 vols.

THE POLITICIAN

MANY THAI WRITERS HAVE BECOME ALMOST
as popular abroad as in Thailand. One of the most famous of
these is the author known as Khamsing Srinawk (pseud. for Lao
Khamhòm). His fiction tells us a great deal about his life, and
about the history of Thailand in the 1950s and 1960s.[1]

Khamsing is a man of Isan, the Northeast, a man born in
some poverty who managed to work himself up in life by his
own efforts, against great odds. He was an assiduous student,
and left home to enter Thammasat University in Bangkok in
the late 1940s. There he supported himself by working as a
writer and reporter for several newspapers. He left Bangkok to
work as a forest ranger in the North (the scene of one of his
stories). He returned to Bangkok in 1956 to resume his career
as a writer of fiction for the newspapers, publishing his first
collection of stories as *Fa bò kan [No Barriers]* in 1958.

All of Khamsing's early stories are set in the rural Northeast
in which he grew up. Most of them have ambiguous endings,
so that the reader is not sure of exactly how the story ends.
Does the hero die at the end of the story or not? Did the hero

---

1. Lao Khamhòm, *The Politician and Other Stories* (Chiang Mai:
Silkworm Books, 2001).

of the story cause the elephant to ram the dwelling-house or not? The author explains that it is not the function of the author to tell the reader what to think, or how to think, but rather to leave readers with the illusion of thinking for him- or herself. There is cynicism in the early stories, but not hopelessness.[2]

The city exists in the early stories, but only by implication. The city is where the "big" people live, the politicians and the royals. It is where evil lives, but it is not necessarily the source of evil. People in Khamsing's villages make bad decisions, but they are not necessarily the dupes of others. Often they are to be admired for their perceptiveness, even when unwitting.

Two stories, written in 1960 and 1962, mark the transition between the simple, rural world of the early stories and the evil, malevolent world of the later ones of the late 1960s. In "The Peasant and the White Man" the protagonist's dog, Somrit, is spoiled by the goodness of the Westerner for whom he works. Here the author is referring allegorically to the prime minister, Sarit, who in a similar way is "spoiled" by his American patrons. In the elliptical story "Owners of Paradise" the author writes about an outdoor privy ruled by khaki-clad flies who seem to stand for the military "owners of paradise."

In real life, the transition was marked by a period that Khamsing spent as a research assistant working for an American university (Cornell) social science project east of Bangkok. He later explained that he was paid too well, being "spoiled by his American patrons." He was able to buy too much agricultural land near his birthplace in the Northeast. He worked too hard,

---

2. For my view on these stories I am especially indebted to the students who read them in my classes, and especially to Tom Judge.

and thereby lost his writer's steam, he explains, and his writing dropped off precipitously.

And indeed, things began to change too quickly from 1957 or 1958. The politics which Khamsing and others could poke fun at grew darker, as government became more efficient but less human. Phibun, who had dominated politics for most of the time from 1933 to 1957, was pushed from power. Phao, well known for his ruthless corruption and his involvement with illegal interests, was supplanted by others. General Sarit Thanarat came to power as prime minister from 1958 to the end of 1963, but died with a record of too much heavy-handed efficiency, too much drinking, too much money, too many mistresses, and too many business enterprises.

By the time Gen. Thanom Kittikhachon succeeded Sarit in December 1963, Thailand already was involved in the Indochina War, and especially in Laos, on the side of the Americans. The stories that Khamsing wrote during this period were less hopeful, and more despairing. Here, there are just three stories from 1969–1970: "Clash" (1969), "Dark Glasses" (1969), and "Sales Reps for the Underworld" (1970). The Thailand of these stories has become more urban, and more awash in cash and corruption.

In "Dark Glasses," a peasant suddenly learns that his beloved daughter has turned to prostitution. In "Clash" the survivors of a horrible bus crash in the countryside are being picked over by robbers for their valuables. In the chilling story of "Sales Reps," a man who has learned of his brother's death in a hospital in the city is besieged by "religious" competing to sell him funeral services.

This sudden turn of the stories to dark and somber scenes unsurprisingly parallels a turn in the author's thinking. Khamsing may have been encouraged by the apparent end of military rule in 1973, but his hopes seem to have been dashed by the horrible events of 1976, when the military came back to power amid terrible bloodshed and violence, and began an ominous turn to the Right.

Khamsing himself hardly was immune from these developments. In a conversation with this author many years ago, he explained what happened to him in this period. His "too-large" farm was located in Nakhon Ratchasima province, in the impoverished Northeast. He despaired at the government's callous indifference to the plight of poor peasant farmers, and saw government as much more solicitous of urban needs than of rural poverty, and far too dominated by the military. He joined the communist insurgents in the jungle, which was not far from the Northeast in which had grown up. He was put to work doing that which he knew best, which was writing. His efforts were rejected for not being sufficiently directive: he should, he was told, tell people what to do, while he preferred to subtly lead people to make up their own minds. Ultimately he left the insurgent movement and returned to rural life.

If we look back at his stories and ask whether they might suggest the subsequent shape of his life, as one of our undergraduate students did some years ago, we can glimpse the best of the qualities which long have distinguished intellectual life in Thailand. In a way, it reminds me of the best of those qualities so distinctive of the generation which founded the Bangkok kingdom more than two hundred years ago. That is, they had at base a knowledge that the world is a dangerous and challenging place. But they also knew that human intelligence was equal to the task of mastering and shaping it. Khamsing constantly showed a similar faith in his fellow human beings. That is, he showed a faith in the ability of his fellow humans to do the right thing; but he also felt that it was not his task to tell people what to do, which would be arrogant, but rather it was his task to encourage people to look at the world and draw their own conclusions.

PAST, PRESENT, AND FUTURE

SOMETIMES, THE PAST SPEAKS MORE PRESCIENTLY about the future than the present. The past is simpler and clearer than the present. Perhaps that's why novelists who write about the past are read so eagerly and profoundly. Two of the many novelists who have written about Thailand so compellingly are historical novelists who have written about the 'thirties and 'forties. These are two prize-winning novelists, "Botan," who writes about Chinese immigrants,[1] and Khampoon Boonthawee, who writes about his childhood in the Northeast long ago.[2]

The rhetorical device used by "Botan" (pseudonym for Supha Lüsiri) is that the book is based upon letters, intercepted by Thai police, from a new immigrant from China to his relatives back home from the 1940s to the 1970s. The premise of the book is in fact questionable, as the Thai police are said to have lacked the relevant linguistic expertise.

---

1. Botan (pseud.), *Letters from Thailand*, tr. Susan Fulop Morell (Bangkok: D. K. Book House, 1977; Chiang Mai: Silkworm Books, 2002).

2. Kampoon Boontawee, *A Child of the Northeast*, tr. Susan Fulop Kepner (Bangkok: Editions Duangkamol, 1988). Despite the name change, the translator of both is the same woman, who is a superb translator.

In writing about these novels, I have benefited greatly from reading the review of both (and others) by Richard West, "Royal Family Thais," *The New York Review*, January 30, 1992, pp. 35–37.

The late 1940s were in fact the last time that immigration from China could proceed unfettered, as the conclusion of the China civil war in 1949 ended legal immigration. The hero of the book, Tan Suang U, began his life in Thailand working in the retail trade in Bangkok. He gradually prospered to the point where he became a shop owner, and married his former employer's daughter. He soon had several children, his favorite among whom was a daughter. The daughter ended up marrying a Thai man, and Suang U ended up living with them, making his peace with his adopted country.

Letters from Thailand is an exceedingly good read, funny and perceptive. What makes it particularly memorable is that, better than most academic efforts, it focuses on what is one of the central issues of modern Thai history. We are reminded that, only seventy years ago, Chinese constituted 12 percent of the population of Siam. An academic friend and I sometimes argue whether it will take another three generations, or only two, for there to be no Chinese left in Thailand. While many of its neighboring countries have known bloody ethnic conflict in recent years, there has been virtually none in Thailand. I remember that, barely forty years ago, it was common to see people, particularly women, dressed in Chinese fashion, in what we would call "black pajamas." Nowadays the "black pajamas" are gone, replaced by *haute couture* and pedal-pushers and blue jeans. The shopkeepers in the Seven Eleven and the shopping center may be Chinese in their ancestry, but to look at them there would be few clues to that fact. Whatever the Thai society of the future may be, it will not be Chinese in culture, nor, in some important ways, will it be Thai. It will be a blend of numerous ingredients, including Chinese.

One of those important ingredients is represented by the second of those novels, *A Child of the Northeast*. In this novel,

Kampoon does not focus directly on any of the momentous changes of the past seventy years. Instead he zeroes in on what might objectively be one bad year in the 1930s in the life of a typical eight-year-old boy, Koon, living in what has invariably been termed the "impoverished" Northeast. It seems like the whole book takes us from one meal to another, through a very difficult year. Readers can be reminded here of what few of us know firsthand, what it is like to be hungry and poor. Viewed from outside, we might have expected the novel to be depressing. It is not. It is amusing and uplifting. The translator, Susan Fulop Kepner, reminds us that the novel "is the simplest of tales, celebrating the most essential aspects of human life: survival, hope, loyalty and love."[3]

One cannot read *A Child of the Northeast* without gaining respect for the neglected farmers of the Northeast; and we learn that Kampoon's novel has gained a permanent place in the consciousness of Thai. In the process, "Lao" of the Northeast have become an accepted part of the society, just as Lao food has become a popular part of the diet of many city-dwellers, and Northeastern migrants have become part of local society almost everywhere.

The two novels mentioned here won major international awards at the two ends of the 1970s. Like other literary prize winners, they tell us something profoundly important about what has happened to the society that has come to appreciate both novels. Both underline the way in which the society has become more inclusive—inclusive of Chinese, inclusive of Northeasterners.

3. *Child of the Northeast*, p. 8.

SIAM IN MIND

THIS BOOK BEGAN WITH A STATEMENT ABOUT how "intellectual history" is simply a history of human thought, not the thought of élites but the thought of very ordinary human beings. In the preceding pages, we have had occasion to meet a wide variety of people, only a few of whom were kings or high-ranking nobles.

I have been concerned in these pages to present brief pictures of a wide variety of people. Some of the chief arguments with which I have been concerned, however, probably have fallen through the cracks, or have remained unnoticed, so let me reiterate them here.

In the first few chapters ("Silver Bullet" and "Relics"), kings and their advisers are at the center of the action; but the real subject is popular religious or quasi-religious belief. Simultaneously, in those chapters and the Ayutthaya chapter that follows, I have been concerned to question the "boundaries" and "frontiers" that are usually used to frame Thai history. Increasingly, I am also concerned to redefine "who" are the subjects of the history of Siam. I am increasingly uncomfortable with the idea that Siam's history is concerned with the history of the "Thai." From the beginning, much attention focuses on the Lao, Chinese, Khmer, and others.

Another focus that appears early and continues through most

of the book is the idea that ordinary people are, by nature, intelligent. It is customary to refer to the people who grow rice and other crops in the countryside as "peasants." I do not like that word: to me, it seems to imply lack of intelligence. It is for that reason that I took great pleasure in the chapter on "Men at War." The point of that and many other chapters is that ordinary people, faced with challenges and puzzles, were perfectly capable of coping with them and solving them.

When I have had occasion to deal with "royal" actions, as in the "Angkor and Sukhothai" and "Linga Forest" chapters, I have taken some pains to "de-royalize" official actions, and to emphasize that such actions usually were the product of the thought and actions of many people.

In a few cases, I don't know the names of the people I am talking about (as with the debate in Chiang Mai in 1827); or in some cases I considered it the better part of valor to refrain from mentioning names.

I have had the most pleasure in writing about people whom we might think of as "artists." Here, I mean the painter of the Wat Phumin murals, the short-story writer in the chapter on "The Politician," the novelists toward the end of the book, and even the "Crazy Bibliophile" in the 1830s! I have also included in this category a number of historians, all of whom are there because they cared about the past (as I do) and tried to write about it.

Obviously, this book has a random quality. It could be a great deal longer, and there easily could be four or five times as many chapters. My intentions are much more modest. All I am trying to do is to demonstrate that all kinds of people in premodern times were "thinkers" whose thought is worth our attention. Here I even mean criminals and people whose thoughts proved to be stupid or misguided. The point is that their thoughts are worth taking seriously.

INDEX OF PROPER NAMES